Rob Gronkowski: The Inspiring Story of One of Football's Greatest Tight Ends

An Unauthorized Biography

By: Clayton Geoffreys

Table of Contents

Foreword

Rob Gronkowski has had an illustrious football career to date. As one of Tom Brady's favorite teammates to turn to in crunch time, Gronkowski, often known as just Gronk, has smashed previous league records including becoming the first tight end in NFL history to lead the league in receiving touchdowns. Few tight ends who have played the game professionally have achieved many of the milestones Gronk has already amassed. Thank you for downloading *Rob Gronkowski: The Inspiring Story of One of Football's Greatest Tight Ends*. In this unauthorized biography, we will learn Rob Gronkowski's incredible life story and impact on the game of football. Hope you enjoy and if you do, please do not forget to leave a review!

Also, check out my website at claytongeoffreys.com to join my exclusive list where I let you know about my latest books. To thank you for your purchase, you can go to my site to download a free copy of *33 Life Lessons: Success Principles, Career Advice & Habits of Successful People*. In the book, you'll learn from some of the greatest thought leaders of different industries on what it takes to become successful and how to live a great life.

Cheers,

Clayton Geoffreys

Visit me at www.claytongeoffreys.com

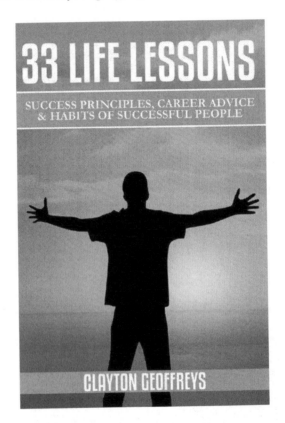

Introduction

Just who is Rob Gronkowski? He may only be 27 years old, but he is already a six-year NFL veteran, two-time Super Bowl Champion, four-time Pro Bowler, party animal, and savvy businessman. New England Patriots fans had no idea who Gronkowski was when the team drafted him in the second round back in 2010. Six years later, they believe he is on pace to become one of the greatest tight ends in NFL history. As much as fans of other teams hate the Patriots, they always concede to this fact. Gronkowski is an awesome physical specimen who terrorizes opposing defenses and gives defensive coordinators consistent nightmares. Watching him do his famous "Gronk Spike" in the end zone after a touchdown has become a regular occurrence.

Fans and experts alike always wonder what makes Rob Gronkowski an elite athlete. Moreover, they would like to know more about the man whose notorious partying ways are always viral on social media. What many do not know is that Gronkowski's emergence from being relatively unknown to an NFL Pro Bowler has been far from easy. He had to endure the aches and pains – both literally and figuratively – a regular person goes through to achieve success. An in-depth look at his life both on and off the field will give the reader a clearer picture of who this perplexing yet outgoing person is.

The reader will know more about Gronkowski's youth in his hometown of Amherst, N.Y., and his home life with his four brothers – a home life that had its share of ups and downs. Gronkowski's humble beginnings will also explain why he is very committed to fitness and health, and remains so to this day despite the many temptations a professional athlete has, some of which he partakes in. He also faced adversity at a very young age dating back to his high school years, despite being a star in basketball and football. As successful as he is now with his fitness business, "The Gronk Bus," his Super Bowl titles, the Gronk Nation Youth Foundation, etc., Gronkowski demonstrated how resilient he is when his journey continued at the University of Arizona and with the New England Patriots.

Many think that Rob Gronkowski is just a rich athlete who likes to party all the time. As the reader will discover in the next few chapters, this will prove to be just a small part of the New England Patriots tight end's persona.

Chapter 1: Childhood and Early Life

Robert James "Rob" Gronkowski was born on May 14, 1989, in Amherst, New York. His parents are Gordon (nicknamed "Gordy") and Diane Gronkowski. He is the fourth of five boys. His brothers are Gordy, Jr., Dan, Chris, and Glenn, in that order.[i]

Athleticism runs in the Gronkowski bloodline through a combination of Polish and American heritage. Rob's great-grandfather, Ignatius, suited up for the United States' men's cycling team in the 1924 Paris Olympics. His grandfather, Ignatius, Jr., was a bodybuilder at one point. He made a living as a liquor salesperson. He had a drinking issue, which got in the way of his relationship with his sons, Gordy and Glenn.

When Glenn got fed up with his father's antics, he would lock himself up in his room and read books all day long. As for Gordy, he would take to the streets and fight people and steal things. He said that being an idiot growing up was his way of making people notice him.

Gordy had always been determined to pursue an athletic career. He was a star player on the West Seneca West Senior High School football team. In spite of his potential, many Division I schools did not recruit him seriously. In his senior year, Gronkowski and a friend boarded a Greyhound bus bound for

California. Gronkowski paid $240 for the bus ticket, which was a very steep price at the time. It occurred shortly after the deadly blizzard which hit Upstate New York in 1977. He had one goal in mind: he wanted to show several college football coaches his potential. The Long Beach State 49ers eventually offered him a scholarship. He went back to the Buffalo area satisfied with knowing he had accomplished his goal.

However, fate had different ideas.

When Gronkowski went back home, he played baseball with his friend Dennis Hartman. Syracuse University recruited the latter. It just so happened the school's defensive line coach also attended the game. Gronkowski's athleticism impressed him so much that he offered him a tryout. The rest, as they say, is history. Gronkowski decided to take up the Syracuse Orangemen's (now known as the Syracuse Orange) offer instead.[ii]

He became an offensive lineman for Syracuse. He started for the Orangemen for three years at guard. His entire college career lasted from 1977 until 1981.

Gronkowski met a girl named Diane in a bar during his college days. They kept running into each other every year at a particular bar and knew it was a sign. Gordy and Diane married after he graduated from Syracuse.

Shortly afterward, the now-defunct United States Football League (USFL) and Canadian Football League (CFL) tried to recruit him. He decided not to pursue a professional football career after a spate of injuries – shoulder, knee, and ankles – took their toll on him.

Several years later, he became the vice president of Superior Lubricants, a company distributing lubricants to clients in the automotive and government sectors. Gronkowski told *Esquire Magazine* he "took that company from $1 million to $18 million." He and his brother Glenn started G&G Fitness – a fitness equipment store – in 1990. They wanted to put up a store of its kind in the Western New York area.

Gordy Gronkowski, Sr. resigned from Superior Lubricants in 1997 so that he could run his fitness business on a full-time basis. The company has made significant process since then. Fifteen branches in New York, Pennsylvania, and Ohio as of 2011 attest to this fact.

To this very day, Gordy Gronkowski, Sr. keeps himself in tip-top shape in his mid-fifties. He has not skipped a week of working out for more than 40 years.[iii] He furnished his basement with approximately $80,000 worth of home gym equipment. There is a machine for each muscle group: pull-up bars, a bench press, a leg press, and much more. He even has a rowing machine and treadmill for cardiovascular exercise. The Gronkowski patriarch works out six days a week.

Rob and his brothers eventually inherited their passion for fitness from their dad. Gordy, Jr. was a baseball player for Jacksonville University. He stands 6'6" and weighs 250 lbs. The Anaheim Angels (now known as the Los Angeles Angels) selected him in the 49th round of the 2006 MLB draft. According to Baseball-Reference.com, he played first base for several minor league teams in the Pioneer League, Frontier League, Midwest League, and Canadian-American Association League. Among the teams he played for from 2006-2011 were the Orem Owlz, Southern Illinois Miners, Cedar Rapids Kernels, Lake Erie Crushers, Gateway Grizzlies, and Worcester Tornadoes. The highest level he reached was Single-A with the Kernels.[iv] He never made it to the Angels' MLB roster.

The second Gronkowski sibling is Dan, who stands 6'5" and weighs 255 lbs. He was a Maryland Terrapins tight end. The Detroit Lions made him the 255th overall selection in the seventh round of the 2009 NFL draft.[v] He also played for the Denver Broncos, New England Patriots, and Cleveland Browns.

He played in a total of 21 NFL games. His most successful campaign was in 2010 with the Broncos. He suited up in 12 games with four starts, recording eight receptions for 65 yards.

The third Gronkowski brother is Chris. He attended the University of Maryland just like his older brother Dan, but transferred to the University of Arizona as a redshirt sophomore in 2007. Chris Gronkowski played fullback for both the Maryland Terrapins and Arizona Wildcats. He would play the same position in the NFL when he signed with the Dallas Cowboys as an undrafted free agent in 2010. He made an impact in his rookie year, totaling seven receptions for 35 yards and a touchdown in 14 games for Dallas.

He would appear in a combined 21 games for the Indianapolis Colts and Denver Broncos in the next two seasons. Unfortunately, he sustained an injury during the San Diego Chargers' training camp before the 2013 NFL season. He eventually agreed to an injury settlement with the team.[vi]

The youngest of the Gronkowski brood is Glenn, whose nickname is "Goose." He is four years younger than Rob, stands almost 6'3", and weighs 238 lbs. He currently plays fullback and tight end for the Kansas State Wildcats. He recorded five receptions for 76 yards and 11 carries for 45 yards in the 2014 NCAA season.[vii]

In the 2016 NFL Combine, Glenn Gronkowski ran the 40-yard dash in 4.71 seconds, lifted 17 repetitions of 225 pounds in the bench press and recorded a vertical jump of 33.0 inches and a broad jump of 120.0 inches. He also ran the three-cone drill in 7.10 seconds, the 20-yard shuttle in 4.45 seconds, and the 60-yard shuttle in 11.95 seconds. [viii]

As good an athlete as he is, he still went undrafted in 2016. Maybe he will get his shot at playing for an NFL team just like his brother Rob someday. In a December 2015 interview with *Vanity Fair Magazine*'s Bruce Weber, Gordy Gronkowski, Sr. said he "coached each of my sons either in hockey or baseball, and they loved it."[ix] He said he would prefer all five of his boys to finish an activity once they started doing it. For instance, if one of them chose to play the trumpet, they should end the year doing so.

The eldest Gronkowski always stressed the importance of academics over athletics. "Hey, school's first no matter what. Get educated, and then the sports," he said. He emphasized that his goal from the get-go was to get all five Gronkowski boys through college with an athletic scholarship.

Gordy Gronkowski, Sr. did not allow his children to play organized football or do strength training in middle school. He believed that doing so would place them on the receiving end of mediocre coaching. At the same time, he was concerned these activities might burn them out and wear their bodies down at a young age.

He took on a more lenient stance not too long afterward.

When the boys reached puberty, Gordy Gronkowski, Sr. told them they need to begin a strict training regimen if they want to pursue an athletic career. Rob was already in the eighth grade around this time. The eldest son, Gordy, Jr., refused at first. However, he saw his younger sibling Danny packing on lean muscle and becoming more athletic. Gordy, Sr. said it was at that moment when his younger namesake decided to train, too. Chris got in on the act, and so did Rob. Their dad compared the phenomenon to "a virus."

Once all the Gronkowski boys caught this so-called "virus," Gordy Gronkowski, Sr. eased them into a training routine. He forbade them from lifting anything too heavy or doing anything extreme like lifting to failure. Every exercise was precise: three sets of 15 repetitions. An example of a routine he taught them was squatting. He first showed them how to do this using a broom handle. After that, they used an 18-lb. bar and then an Olympic bar. He increased the resistance in 2.5-lb. increments. He made sure to guide them for the first two years of their training.

"What I always preached was," Gordy, Sr. told Men's Fitness, "don't come down here to throw weight on and be an idiot and show off for a girl... Your joints and growth plates are wide open right now, and I don't want you getting hurt. Back in my day, it was, 'no pain, no gain.' That's a bunch of b------t. I worked out three hours a day and ripped my joints apart."

With this, Rob Gronkowski gave credit to his father for introducing him and his brothers to a fit lifestyle.

"Our dad introduced us to all of it," he said. "The weights, eating healthy, all that good stuff. He introduced it, got on us every once in a while, and left it up to us if we wanted to do it. And seeing my older brothers do it right in front of me, I wanted to do it because I looked up to them. I caught right onto the program."

He described his family's basement gym as a "mini full weight room." If he and his brothers needed to exercise a particular body part, they had a piece of equipment which would fill that need. Rob Gronkowski considered it a luxury not too many families had.[x]

He believes he got his determination from that point of his life.

"Just getting it implanted in me as a kid," he told *Providence Journal's* Mark Daniels in October 2014. I feel growing up like that is making me who I am now. Keeping all the hard work going, the success going. I feel like that's where it starts – in the weight room to get you strong and get you ready."

Gordy Gronkowski, Sr. would also hurl tennis balls at his sons from a close distance. He believed that this would toughen them up and make them more determined. When Rob turned 13 years old, he caught the tennis balls from as close as 12 yards out.[xi]

Now that all five Gronkowski boys are grown up, one would find it difficult to imagine how their father keeps track of even the minutest details of their lives.

For Gordy Gronkowski, Sr., this is not a problem.

Today, the 56-year-old dad knows each of his son's weight. "Robby's 265, I think Danny's 260 right now, Gordy's close to 250, Chris is at 245, and Goose right now is about 238," he told *Esquire Magazine's* Chris Jones in June 2014. That adds up to a total of 1,258 lbs. for all five sons.[xii]

As good as it was for the Gronkowski brood to live a fit lifestyle, it also had its downsides.

The five brothers were always competing against each other. Whether it was playing football or hockey in Western New York, they would go at it. If someone lost, the winner would let him hear about it. If a Gronkowski brother fared poorly in a Little League game, the others would give him a hard time once he got home.

As time went by, this fierce competition carried over into the weight room in the Gronkowski garage. They gave bragging rights to whoever could squat or bench press the heaviest.

As the second youngest of the brood, Rob Gronkowski received a fair share of humiliation from his brothers.

"His brothers used to beat him up royally," Gordy, Sr. said. "And he just used to get back in it again. Robby just loved the pain. They used to give that kid so many Charley horses. They would pin him down and keep nailing him on the legs and arms, and he'd get up, and they'd go right back after him again, and he just loved it."

Despite the fact his brothers gave Rob Gronkowski a hard time, he knew it brought out the best in him.

"Competing with my brothers at such a young age gave me a huge competitive advantage," he revealed.

Rob Gronkowski's dad agrees. He attributes his son's greatness to his fearlessness. "That's what makes Rob great today," Gordy, Sr. beams. "He's got no fear. It started out from the get-go, the brawling. The kid just endured pain."

For her part, Diane Gronkowski did not find it easy to raise five competitive boys.

The family moved into their new house on New Road in Amherst, N.Y. in 2002. As the Gronkowski brothers grew up and became more enamored with their fitness regimen, their mother provided them with muscle-building food such as chicken and steak. She also served them plenty of fresh vegetables and almost no junk food.

Because the couple had five boys, it was no surprise their already massive appetite grew bigger as they trained. The Gronkowskis needed four freezers in their household – one in the kitchen and three more in the garage. According to Gordy, Sr., the weekly grocery bill was as much as $500 to $600. The brothers also needed to have at least 2.5 gallons of milk daily.

Gordy Gronkowski, Sr. did not consider himself to be a strict disciplinarian. However, he had to take on that role when things got a bit out of hand. He told *Vanity Fair's* Bruce Weber in December 2015, "All the boys got at least one good whupping and soap in the mouth." Diane Gronkowski would call him while he was at work if they acted up. When their father got home, he would – in his way of putting it – "raise hell."

Mr. Gronkowski even said it got so bad one time that his wife had to drop their kids off at his office showroom. He knew back then that raising five boys was no easy task. His wife would even say she would still be catching up on sleep 20 years after they had all grown up.

Diane singles out Rob as the son who gave her the hardest time.

"He was always tough on me," she told ESPN Boston's Jackie MacMullan in January 2012. "Of the five of them, he gave me the hardest time. He was always pushing, always challenging."[xiii]

Despite the occasional struggles which come with raising five boys, Gordy Gronkowski cherishes each of their achievements.

Aside from his high-end home gym, he also put up five trophy cabinets in his basement – one assigned to each son. He arranged them according to their birth dates: Gordy, Jr., Dan,

Chris, Rob, and Glenn a.k.a. "Goose." He proudly displays an estimated 500 trophies for his visitors to see. It comes as no surprise Rob has the most. His trophy cabinet includes a football he caught for his first touchdown as a New England Patriots rookie tight end in 2010.

Gordy, Sr. now finds himself undoing the damage his five sons inflicted on his house when they were growing up. He has had to retouch scuff marks, patch holes, and repair broken furniture. Dan, who is currently working in his G&G Fitness' marketing department, lives nearby. He would drop by now and then to work out. His brother, Gordy, Jr., also works at their dad's company. The eldest of the Gronkowski brothers lives in Columbus, OH. He manages the stores across the Buckeye State. As for Chris Gronkowski, he and his girlfriend reside in the Dallas area. Their online engraving business is doing better than expected.

Gordy, Sr. and Diane separated in 2005 and eventually divorced a few years later. He gives her credit for raising their five children. He believes this would not have been possible had they not worked well as a team. Gordy, Sr. told *Esquire Magazine* in 2014 Diane could not stand his passion for winning. That was the main reason their relationship fizzled out.

"The wife hated that," he said. "She couldn't stand that I had to win all the time. Even when we played coed volleyball or something, I had to win. She'd say it was just for fun, and I'd say, 'Yeah, isn't it fun winning?'"

He currently has a girlfriend. They do not live in the same house. His new love has five children of her own – one boy and four girls.

Chapter 2: High School Years

Rob Gronkowski attended Williamsville North High School in Western New York for three years. He became a member of the varsity football team in his freshman year. Because of his athletic prowess, he earned a spot as the squad's starting placekicker. Gronkowski eventually played on both sides of the ball in his sophomore and junior seasons as both a tight end and defensive end. In one game, he scored all of his team's points – a fumble recovery for a touchdown, a touchdown catch, and a sack in the end zone for a safety – to secure a playoff berth for his school.

Mike Mammoliti was his head football coach at Williamsville North High School. He marveled at Gronkowski's athleticism.

"It was pretty evident that Rob was a cut above the rest," he said. "Physically, he just had that ability to bend and move and create power better than everybody."

Gronkowski displayed his strength during a game against Williamsville North's rival, North Tonawanda. His team was on their opponent's 16-yard line. It was a fourth-and-2 situation. He and his teammates needed a touchdown for the victory. He told them to give him the ball, and they did.

When Gronkowski caught the ball, he not only scored the goal, he also dragged three opposing players with him. That was how strong he was.

Gronkowski played football, hockey, basketball, and football. His mother Diane would cook his favorite dish, chicken soufflé. He would then eat it inside the van after football on his way to his hockey game. That was one of Rob's traditions – he would eat his meals inside the vehicle in between practices.

One time, Williamsville North's basketball team played a game on the road, and Gronkowski was a member of that team. He remembered dunking the ball in Shaquille-O'Neal-fashion, shattering the backboard.

Gronkowski had it made. He tallied 36 receptions for 648 yards and seven touchdowns in his junior season. On the defensive side of the ball, he wound up with 73 tackles and 6.0 sacks. He went on to earn first-team All-Western New York and second-team All-State honors.[xiv]

However, not everything went smoothly. When Gronkowski was a high school junior, a good number of the students read a crass email regarding one of the teachers. The email address it came from happened to be Gronkowski's. Even though several boys were behind the stunt, the principal still slapped

Gronkowski with a one-game suspension. His mother told ESPN Boston that "it was not anything illegal." She considered it as something that stupid teenagers normally do.

The incident happened to coincide with Gordy, Sr. and Diane's separation. The three older boys had already left the house. Rob's father expanded his fitness equipment business to the Pittsburgh, PA area and brought Rob along with him. His fourth son transferred to the local Woodland Hills High School in 2006. The youngest, Glenn, stayed with Diane in Upstate New York.

Rob Gronkowski did not like the feeling of leaving his mother behind. He remembered how she had always been there for him and his brothers. "It was very tough on Rob," Mammoliti said. "His parents were doing what was best for the family. But he was sad. He walked out with me to my car to say goodbye, and he put his hand on my shoulder. It was so big it draped from one end to the other…He said, 'Coach, I gotta go. I'm so sorry. I don't want to. But I've got to.' I really felt for the kid."

Gronkowski would run into another obstacle shortly afterward.

His father made an off-hand comment to *The Pittsburgh Post-Gazette's* Mike White in an August 11, 2006, phone interview about the reasons behind his son's transfer. He said he owned five G&G Fitness stores in the city and also maintained that Rob wanted to play for a better football program.

"There's just not the quality of football in the state of New York that there is here. We want him to play with good talent around him instead of getting triple-teamed. Here, he blends right in," Gordy Gronkowski, Sr. told White.[xv]

According to an August 2006 report, the Western Pennsylvania Interscholastic Athletic League (WPIAL) ruled Gronkowski ineligible because it ruled he transferred to Woodland Hills High School for athletics. Gronkowski and his family declined to comment to *The Pittsburgh Post-Gazette* on the matter.

However, Gordy Gronkowski, Sr. did tell *The Buffalo News* (via *The Pittsburgh Post-Gazette*) that the media misinterpreted his statement. "The whole thing was a setup," he fumed.[xvi]

At the time, a high school football scouting website ranked his son the second-best tight end in the nation. He had such a sterling reputation that the Arizona Wildcats, Maryland Terrapins, Clemson Tigers, North Carolina Tar Heels, and Ohio State Buckeyes had already given him scholarship offers.

Just three days after the Western Pennsylvania Interscholastic Athletic League made their decision, Rob Gronkowski learned that he could play in Western Pennsylvania after all. The Pennsylvania Interscholastic Athletic Association (PIAA) overturned WPIAL's earlier verdict and declared Rob Gronkowski eligible to play for his new high school.

Craig Lee served as the Gronkowskis' attorney. He told *The Pittsburgh Post-Gazette's* Colin Dunlap that Gordy Gronkowski, Sr. told the truth to Mike White – that football in Pittsburgh is better than in Buffalo. In Lee's words, it was "two guys talking football."

Brad Cashman was the PIAA's executive director at the time. He maintained that he spoke with both Gordy, Sr. and Rob about the situation. They insisted that the media took the older Gronkowski's comments out of context. Cashman was satisfied. Rob Gronkowski was officially a member of the Woodlands Hills High football team.

However, he had to sit out the opening game against Mt. Lebanon on September 1, 2006, as part of the five-game suspension (and not the one-game suspension ESPN Boston reported) stemming from the email incident at Williamsville North in New York State.

Once Gronkowski received clearance to play, many were in awe of him. 247Sports scouting director Barton Simmons was one of them.

"Gronkowski was absolutely one of those guys whom some people looked at and saw an offensive tackle because of his size," he told Bleacher Report's Tyler Donohue in September of 2015. "He probably could have been a first-round pick at offensive tackle if he wanted to do that, but he was just so uniquely talented…You knew he was going to be a force in some capacity. It was just a matter of whether he was going to be a force as a pass-catcher or more of a line-of-scrimmage presence."[xvii]

Woodland Hills High head football coach George Novak remembered the day when he first saw the father-son tandem and thought they were college coaches. He recalls how Rob Gronkowski looked the same he does today when he was 17 years old. He described his new star athlete as "a physical specimen with a big smile on his face."

Gronkowski had an interesting way of introducing himself to his new teammates.

On the first day of training camp, the team was on their lunch break. He made his way toward one of the linebackers who was eating. Gronkowski nonchalantly took his cookie from his tray, bit off a part of it, and then put it back.

His former teammate Rontez Miles remembered Gronkowski fell silent for a while after the prank. Then all of a sudden, he started laughing. Miles considered it a unique way of making an introduction.

Noah Taylor is the younger brother of Jason Taylor, the retired Miami Dolphins defensive end. Gronkowski and the younger Taylor were high school teammates. The latter was in awe of the new kid's phenomenal strength.

"He was the guy who could keep piling weights on the bar, then lift it and make it look like nothing," Taylor said. From there on out, he called Gronkowski "Drago," the powerful Russian opponent of Rocky Balboa from the movie Rocky IV.

Gronkowski's amazing feats of strength on the gridiron would also continue in Pittsburgh.

There was an instance when he blasted through the offensive line and threw the quarterback in his end zone. When Taylor saw it, he came up with a new nickname: "Big Rob."

Gronkowski would not relent. During a game, one of the officials even had to tell Novak and his staff that they needed to take it easier on opposing players.

Taylor and Gronkowski became close. Whenever the latter's father had to go out of town for business, Rob would stay with his teammate. He would also find solace in his mother visiting him on weekends. Diane Gronkowski regularly brought her son his favorite rum cake. Taylor labeled his friend "a mama's boy." Despite Diane's best efforts, Gronkowski still felt homesick. He tried to plead his case with his dad. He wanted to go back to his old high school in Western New York.

It did not happen.

Gronkowski remained at Woodland Hills High for the remainder of the 2006 season where he recorded eight receptions and four touchdowns. Despite the sub-par numbers, he earned many accolades. Among these were SuperPrep All-American, PrepStar All-American, *The Pittsburgh Post-Gazette's* "Fabulous 22," and *The Pittsburgh Post-Gazette's* first-team all-conference.

It turns out a JUGS passing machine was one of the keys to Gronkowski's rapid development as a high school senior.

Woodland Hills High purchased one before Gronkowski's senior year. The Pittsburgh Post-Gazette's Mike White – the same Mike White who interviewed Gronkowski's father before Rob's ineligibility ruling – told Bleacher Report in September 2015 that Gronkowski caught every pass the machine hurled at him in training camp. Even when Novak and the rest of the coaching staff turned up the speed, Gronkowski would still catch the footballs.

Several months after he interviewed Gordy Gronkowski, Sr., Mike White saw Rob Gronkowski at a scrimmage game of basketball. The Woodland Hills tight end impressed the crowd with an array of pre-game dunks. One of those was a 360-degree slam which left everybody in awe.

"When I saw Gronkowski on the court," White told Bleacher Report. "That's when my jaw dropped. I'm watching this guy in warm-ups, and his athleticism was off the charts."

"It's a quarter into the game," White continued. "And I turned to my wife and said, 'See that kid? He's going to be in the NFL.' Did I know he was going to be this good? No, I don't think anybody did."

Gronkowski displayed his tremendous athletic abilities not only on the football field and basketball court but the baseball diamond as well. According to Donohue, he batted cleanup for the squad.

Rob Gronkowski may have been just 17 years old, but he had already given everyone a glimpse of what he was capable of. It was just a small taste of what he could do once he reached the collegiate ranks.

Chapter 3: Recruitment and College Years at Arizona

Even before the 2006 high school football season ended, Rob Gronkowski was already a hot commodity.

According to Bleacher Report, 247Sports rated Gronkowski as a four-star tight end prospect. The website also ranked him as the fourth-best tight end in the nation. What's more is that he placed 84th overall in 247Sports' composite rankings for the 2007 NCAA football season. The likes of the Clemson Tigers, Syracuse Orange, and Ohio State Buckeyes pursued him dating back to his high school days.

Tim Kish is currently the linebacker coach of the Oklahoma Sooners. He has been coaching college football since 1978. He told Bleacher Report's Tyler Donohue that Gronkowski received around "45 to 50 scholarship offers" from various schools. At the time, Kish served as one of the assistants to Arizona Wildcats head football coach Mike Stoops. Kish would also become the driving force behind Gronkowski's recruitment. He recalled the time the prized tight end came over to the university's Tucson campus. He felt that Gronkowski came away impressed with the school and weather. What is more important was that he knew he would be in a situation where he could make an immediate impact. Stoops and Co. employed a high-octane passing attack, and Gronkowski would be right in the middle of it all.

Kish admired Gronkowski's tremendous upside and attitude from the get-go.

"We anticipated he'd be successful," he said. "We just didn't know how good he could be. He's a unique and rare athlete...He's got a tremendous passion to play the game. He's fiery-competitive. Rob doesn't like to lose at anything, but at the same time, he's a happy-go-lucky guy after the game."

247Sports director of scouting Barton Simmons echoed Kish's sentiments. Despite Gronkowski's reputation as a party-goer, Simmons liked the way he managed himself both on and off the field.

"He was a guy who would enjoy the campus visits," Simmons told Bleacher Report. "Pictures would emerge of him with coeds. He'd refer to himself as 'The Big, Bad Gronk' sometimes. The personality was always there, and that was evident from the beginning. In a lot of cases today, his persona would maybe raise some red flags, but he's managed it so well that if anything, it's a positive with him."

For his part, Gordy Gronkowski, Sr. told *Vanity Fair Magazine* in a December 2015 interview that Rob received "something like 65 scholarship offers."

"I asked, 'Where are you going? Syracuse? Ohio State?'" The older Gronkowski said. "He goes, 'University of Arizona.' I asked, 'Why there?'"

Rob Gronkowski's response was one for the ages.

"Dad, if you ever went to a pool party at Arizona, you'd understand," Rob told Gordy, Sr.

Robert James Gronkowski was going to attend the University of Arizona. He made his verbal commitment to the University in January 2007, which coincided with the halfway point of his high school basketball season. Gronkowski averaged a double-

double for Woodland Hills High. Kish and the other Arizona Wildcats coaching staff members were jubilant.

Kish was on vacation in the White Mountains of Northern Arizona when Gordy Gronkowski, Sr. and Rob called him. The Wildcats assistant football coach was chopping wood.

"Probably everybody in the White Mountains could hear me screaming after that conversation," Kish told Bleacher Report. "It was a scream of excitement. We were so thrilled to get him on board. It was huge."

Gronkowski would get right down to business once he took the field for his freshman season at Arizona in the 2007 NCAA football season.

He caught 28 passes and six touchdowns for Arizona. His 28 receptions are the third most in Wildcats school history for tight ends. He set the record for this category during his sophomore season with an astounding 47 receptions (despite missing three games), 15 more than Mark Keel's 32 in 1980. Gronkowski also posted an 18.8 yards-per-catch average as a freshman – the highest on the squad. He set a school record for a tight end with 525 receiving yards on the season.

Gronkowski would continue to earn more accolades. *The Sporting News* named him to its Freshman All-Pac 10 Team for 2007. League coaches also named him as an honorable mention in the All-Pac 10 after his freshman year. His biggest awards that season were his Freshman All-American honors from both *The Sporting News* and Rivals.com.

Gronkowski took his performance to the next level during his sophomore season.

Aside from his school record of 47 receptions for a tight end, he amassed 672 receiving yards and ten touchdowns. Five of them came in his first two games back. Gronkowski caught three touchdown passes in the Wildcats' 48-14 rout of the Washington Huskies on October 4, 2008. It was the highest number of goals he scored in a single game at the college level, per the Arizona Wildcats' official athletics website.

Gronkowski also had at least 109 receiving yards on three occasions. His most impressive outing as a collegian occurred on November 15, 2008, in a 55-45 road loss to Arizona's Pac-10 rivals, the Oregon Ducks. Gronkowski's stat line was 143 yards and one touchdown on 12 receptions.[xviii] Gronkowski earned his second John Mackey National Tight End of the Week Award for the season shortly afterward.

The Arizona Wildcats finished with an 8-5 win-loss record, good enough for fifth in the Pac-10 in 2008. Despite the team's sub-par showing, Gronkowski broke the school's tight end records once the season drew to a close – he became the single-game, season, and career records holder for touchdowns (16), yards (1,197), and receptions (75). *The Associated Press* named him to its All-American third team roster for the 2008 NCAA season. He also made it to the All-Pac-10's first team. Arizona's official athletics website described Gronkowski as "the best tight end in Arizona annals." It also described him as having "the entire package of blocking skill, open-field power and speed, route-running, and catching ability."

Rob Gronkowski became even more of a force as his collegiate career wore on. He even made it to the preliminary watch list for the 2009 Rotary Lombardi Award. According to ArizonaWildcats.com, candidates earned a spot on this list by "earning All-American honors, or by being named to their respective all-conference first team as selected by the conference's head coaches."[xix]

Among the other high-profile college football players who made the list were the Penn State Nittany Lions' NaVorro Bowman, the South Carolina Gamecocks' Jared Cook, the Syracuse

Orange's Arthur Jones, the Alabama Crimson Tide's Rolando McClain, and the Oklahoma State Cowboys' Russell Okung.

Despite the honor, Gronkowski would run into another obstacle just as he did during his high school years in Western New York and Western Pennsylvania.

Arizona Wildcats head football coach Mike Stoops told the media on September 19, 2009, that Gronkowski would sit out the entire season due to a strained back. Stoops broke the news in the aftermath of Arizona's 27-17 road loss to the Iowa Hawkeyes. A September 2009 *Associated Press* report (via ESPN) says the team felt that Gronkowski's back had not made significant progress. He was scheduled to undergo surgery the week after the Wildcats made the announcement.[xx]

In his 2015 autobiography entitled *It's Good to be Gronk* (via an excerpt on MMQB.SI.com released in July 2015), Gronkowski traced his back issue to his first time doing deadlifts.[xxi]

"After spring practice ended in April, I didn't want to lose any momentum," Gronkowski wrote. "So I lifted weights in the gym with (Gronkowski's older brother) Chris like a madman. One day, the guys in the gym were all doing deadlifts. I had never done deadlifts before as part of my training, but one of the team strength trainers was supervising it, so I figured, 'Why not?' I should have paced myself and stayed at lighter weights, but I got all macho, maxed it out, and went too heavy. On the last set, I felt something pop in my back. It didn't feel right, but I finished lifting through the pain. I didn't think anything of it."

"All through April and May I kept lifting and running," Gronkowski continued. "By July I had mad back pain, and at the end of the month, it was so bad that the nerves in my legs weren't working. My legs felt like they were 500 lbs. each, and I couldn't jump or run. I finally told my dad and trainers."

Gronkowski underwent an MRI. He said that the results were not encouraging: it was a badly ruptured disk that severely affected the nerves in his spine. In his book, he mentioned that he asked several doctors for their opinions. He sought the advice of Dr. Robert Watkins, a spine specialist based in California. Dr. Watkins suggested Gronkowski undergo physical therapy to alleviate the searing back pain. If that did not work, he would need to have surgery. The Arizona tight end said he could suffer permanent leg damage if his spinal cord nerves did not heal.

Before the injury, Gronkowski said he knew he would be "the best tight end in the country." He felt he was in peak physical condition during spring practices.

It was also an exciting time for the Gronkowski family.

The Detroit Lions selected Gronkowski's second-oldest brother Dan in the 2009 NFL draft. Rob and his third-oldest sibling, Chris, were teammates at Arizona. The former laid out their plan in his autobiography: he and Chris would join Dan in the National Football League after the 2009 NCAA football season. Chris would declare for the draft after his senior season while Rob would do the same after his junior season at Arizona.

Rob Gronkowski also revealed in his book that his dad advised him to take on a disability insurance policy for $4 million before his junior season with the Wildcats. It stemmed from the fact that Gronkowski was one of the most prolific and highly-touted tight ends in the country.

"I knew better than to second-guess him when it came to business, so I took his advice and appreciated him buying that policy for me," Gronkowski said.

And then all of a sudden, he sustained a major back injury.

He now had a decision to make. He could either work himself back into game shape or retire at the age of 19 with $4 million. Gronkowski said he could earn $160,000 every year on a four percent annual interest rate. He did not have to spend a penny from the $4 million he had at his disposal.

Gronkowski had his doubts about going for the latter option. He still set his heart on playing football and making a living playing the game he loved.

"But I didn't want the easy money," he said. "I wanted to earn it by playing football. Maybe a lot of people would take the money and run, but I looked at it as quitting. I was happy playing football, and didn't want to give that up."

Robert James Gronkowski was wise beyond his 19 years of age.

With that, he decided to take Dr. Watkins' advice and undergo physical therapy. Arizona Wildcats trainer Randy Cohen would facilitate his recovery. Under Cohen's guidance, the pain in Gronkowski's back began to disappear. He felt his strength and agility coming back. Gronkowski ran some routes during the Wildcats' second practice. While doing so, he felt the pain and numbness return. He knew his season was officially over.

Gronkowski proceeded to step two of Dr. Watkins' intervention plan: surgery. Gordy, Sr. accompanied his son to California for the procedure. The doctor explained to them that parts of the younger Gronkowski's ruptured disk pressed against his spinal cord nerves, resulting in nerve damage. Rob Gronkowski said that even if the surgery were successful, the nerves would have to heal on their own. If this did not happen correctly, Gronkowski would suffer permanent leg damage.

For three weeks after the procedure, he did not do anything strenuous. He had to be careful with his back. "Every wrong move sent sharp pain up my spine and down my legs," Gronkowski quipped.

Despite his situation, he remained unfazed. Not being able to party or hang out with his friends could have made him feel desperate. Not Rob Gronkowski.

In his autobiography, he said his disposition carried him through this tough time.

"I think it's because I'm such a big kid at heart and always joking around that I'm able to keep the pressure from getting to me," Gronkowski declared. "There's no reason you can't work hard, do what you are supposed to, and still have fun in the process."

Gronkowski was also fortunate to be in a football program such as Arizona's. He said had he gone through the same situation at some other schools, the people around him would have forgotten about him. The Wildcats were different. Cohen picked up from where he left off in the rehab process. He became a key figure not only in saving Gronkowski's college football career, but also in a future career in the professional ranks.

Three months after Gronkowski injured his back, he was making significant progress. By December 2009, he was already doing some light running.

It was also during this time when he had to make his all-important decision. Would he retire, stay in Arizona, or turn pro? Gronkowski also came up with the idea of training for the 2010 NFL Scouting Combine in Indianapolis in February. It was a win-win situation: if he fared well, he would declare for the 2010 NFL draft. Otherwise, he could always return to Arizona for his senior year.

Gronkowski had to decide by January 15. It was the deadline for juniors to declare for the pros. He also got some good news from Dr. Watkins. His ruptured disk was now fully healed, and he could not find any traces of nerve damage. Gronkowski said the turn of events did not surprise him one bit. Sitting out his junior season made him sad, but the fact he would be able to play football again made him feel invincible.

Now that Dr. Watkins had given Gronkowski a clean bill of health, the latter had to work harder than he ever had. The period between December 15, 2009, and January 15, 2010, was a critical one. He had to be in the best shape of his life if he wanted to impress general managers, coaches, and scouts in the following year's NFL Scouting Combine.

Gronkowski started working with trainer Pete Bommarito in Miami in December 2009. The latter said they trained from 6 a.m. to 7 p.m. daily. Bommarito gave Gronkowski the full arsenal: pool work, cardiovascular exercise, strength training, massages, and all sorts of therapy. Gordy Gronkowski, Sr. was on the phone with Bommarito every day to get a progress report on his son.

Rob Gronkowski epitomized the perfect student – he was always present and on time. He followed Bommarito's nutrition plan to the letter. He felt grateful because his brother Chris accompanied him to Florida. Having him around kept the pressure off Rob Gronkowski.

Two days before the January 15 deadline, Pete Bommarito told Gronkowski that his rehab enabled him to reach the average fitness levels of an NFL tight end. He even had a chance to reach the above-average level. At that point, Gronkowski knew he did not want the $4 million worth of insurance money. He wanted to be an NFL player. He made it official: he would declare for the 2010 NFL draft.

Chapter 4: Scouting Combine and 2010 NFL Draft

Twenty-year-old Robert James Gronkowski was determined to become an NFL player from the get-go.

Gronkowski wore the number 11 at the 2010 NFL Scouting Combine, an event which is held in February every year at the Indianapolis Colts' Lucas Oil Stadium. NFL general managers, head coaches, and scouts convene during this annual gathering to get a feel for what pro football prospects can do before drafting them two months later. They had to display their athletic prowess in front of these executives. Among the events that these would-be NFL rookies participated in were the 40-yard dash, bench press, 20-yard split, 10-yard split, vertical jump, broad jump, shuttle, and the three-cone drill.

Gronkowski would participate together with the likes of the Georgia Bulldogs defensive tackle Geno Atkins, Tennessee Volunteers free safety Eric Berry, Oklahoma Sooners quarterback Sam Bradford, Iowa Hawkeyes offensive tackle Bryan Bulaga, Virginia Tech Hokies free safety Kam Chancellor, and Texas Longhorns cornerback Earl Thomas.[xxii]

The official NFL website featured an analysis of Gronkowski heading into the 2010 NFL Scouting Combine:

"Gronkowski made an immediate impact when he arrived at the University of Arizona and has been a standout tight end when he has been healthy enough to stay on the field. Unfortunately, he has missed a total of 16 games over the past two years due to injuries or illness. He has an elite combination of size, speed, and athleticism for the position and while he lacks great downfield speed, he can be an effective receiver at virtually all levels of the passing tree. He is a tough, no-nonsense type of blocker, but still needs some work on his blocking techniques. If he can stay healthy, he could provide a team with a quality starting tight end."[xxiii]

Unfortunately, Gronkowski was not healthy enough to perform the running drills at the 2010 NFL Scouting Combine, which was due to the back injury he sustained the previous year. Even when Dr. Robert Watkins declared Gronkowski's ruptured disk to have fully healed, the latter was not at his physical peak in February 2010.

However, Gronkowski still took part in the bench press. He lifted a 225-lb. barbell 23 times, per Boston.com's Albert Breer.[xxiv]

The New England Patriots showed a keen interest in Rob Gronkowski during the 2010 NFL Scouting Combine in Indianapolis, IN. Arizona Wildcats head football coach Mike Stoops recommended him highly to Patriots head coach Bill Belichick and his staff. For his part, Belichick marveled at Gronkowski's attitude, aggressiveness, and playmaking abilities.[xxv]

On the other hand, the Indianapolis Colts were not as interested in Gronkowski. Former Colts president and general manager Bill Polian (who now serves as an ESPN NFL analyst) told SiriusXM NFL Radio the prized tight end was not on the team's radar. After all, the Colts still had 2009 Pro Bowl tight end Dallas Clark – one of the most prolific tight ends in both franchise and NFL history.

At the time of the 2010 NFL Scouting Combine, Belichick told ESPN Boston's Mike Reiss that he got word from the Patriots' team physicians that Gronkowski's health had improved. The Patriots became even more intrigued.

"When our doctors said he was okay, that was the point (we became comfortable)," Belichick said. "We go on their evaluations and recommendations. We have a deal: I don't diagnose with the players, and they don't call plays."

"He's a big guy and has a big frame," Belichick continued. "A hard matchup for a defensive back. He just boxes them out, and they stuck it in there to him, and he's just a hard guy to cover."

Reiss said the Patriots scheduled a private workout with Gronkowski before the 2010 NFL draft in April of that year. He exceeded their expectations during the session. Belichick and Co. were confident that his rehabilitation was on schedule, and he still had a skillset which made him one of college football's best tight ends.

Belichick showed his admiration for one of Gronkowski's key traits: he also had the ability to split out wide. This meant he could run precise receiving routes on both the strong and weak sides.

Another team which eyed Gronkowski was the Baltimore Ravens.

His agent, Drew Rosenhaus, refuted reports that said NFL teams "red-flagged" him because of stenosis. This is when the spine narrows, resulting in numbness and even paralysis.

"Every team I have talked to says there are no concerns about his back," Rosenhaus told *The Baltimore Sun's* Jamison Hensley, "He passed his physical at the combine. There are no red flags on him. He is ready to go. The back is not a factor. There's no issue."[xxvi]

That being the case, an insider told *The Sporting News* (via *The Baltimore Sun*) the Ravens could end up drafting somebody like Gronkowski or Georgia Tech Yellow Jackets wide receiver Demaryius Thomas.

Ravens head coach John Harbaugh confirmed to MASN Sports' Dan Kolko two years later that they were indeed interested in Gronkowski.

"We were very interested in Rob," Harbaugh said. "There were medical concerns, but we loved him – loved him as a player, loved him as a guy. We were pretty certain he was going to be a good player, and he's exceeded our expectations."[xxvii]

At this point, it was evident that Gronkowski had made enough of an impact in his two years at Arizona. Despite sitting out the entire 2009 NCAA football season due to a back injury, his determination carried him through. He had limited physical prowess during the 2010 NFL Scouting Combine in February.

However, he more than made up for that with an impressive Pro Day performance at the University of Arizona on March 27, 2010.

According to CBS Sports (via PatsPulpit.com), he participated in all the position drills. He impressed observers with his catching and route running abilities and recorded just two drops.[xxviii]

In his 2010 Pro Day, Rob Gronkowski ran the 40-yard dash in 4.65 seconds with the wind and 4.73 seconds against the wind. He recorded a vertical jump of 33.5 inches and a broad jump of 9 feet and 11 inches. He also ran the short shuttle in 4.47 seconds and the three-cone drill in 7.18 seconds.

Chris Gronkowski – the third of the brood – also participated in the 2010 Pro Day at the University of Arizona. He ran the 40-yard dash in 4.72 seconds with the wind and 4.71 seconds against it. He fared slightly better than Rob in the short shuttle with a time of 4.40 seconds.

Chris Gronkowski revealed in his brother Rob's 2014 book, *Growing Up Gronk*, that the two of them went beyond their limits on that particular Pro Day.

"We killed it that day," he said. We caught every pass and ran so hard we were about to throw up. We really got after it. Rob had on his blocking pads, and I ran him at full speed, then we switched. I was trying to drill him as hard as I could."[xxix]

NFL teams such as the New England Patriots and Baltimore Ravens were interested in Rob Gronkowski. All he needed to do was wait and see who would select him on draft day.

It turned out Gronkowski would strut his wares in the Northeast.

His big day came on April 22, 2010, the first day of the 2010 NFL draft at Radio City Music Hall in New York City. In his 2015 autobiography *It's Good to be Gronk*, he said that the New England Patriots called him. They had just traded their sixth-round selection to the Oakland Raiders so they could move up two spots from 44th to 42nd in the draft sequence. New England would select the Arizona stalwart. He would be the second tight end drafted behind the Oklahoma Sooners' Jermaine Gresham (whom the Cincinnati Bengals made the 21st overall pick). When Gronkowski received the news, he was elated.

"I was as emotional as I've ever been in my life," he said.

He hugged and kissed his father, Gordy, Sr., and his mother, Diane. A few moments later, NFL commissioner Roger Goodell took to the podium and made it official. Robert James Gronkowski was now a member of the New England Patriots.

Gronkowski went up on stage and wore his Patriots cap. He also brought a Patriots helmet with him. He then shook hands with

Commissioner Goodell. As he made his way to the opposite side of the stage, NFL Network's Deion Sanders took him aside for an interview. Gronkowski said he was very emotional during that moment. "This is the greatest moment of my life. This is unbelievable," Gronkowski said.

After the interview, Gronkowski celebrated with his family. He chest bumped his brothers along the way. He also wore his Patriots helmet and screamed in sheer delight at the television camera. The celebration continued until the New England Patriots called again and politely asked him to get off the stage.

A brand new chapter in Rob Gronkowski's life was about to begin.

Chapter 5: Gronkowski's NFL Career

Just a week after the New England Patriots drafted him, Rob Gronkowski was still excited. He knew he would fit perfectly in Bill Belichick's system.

"I just felt like it was always my dream to play in the NFL," Gronkowski told the *Amherst Bee*'s Patrick J. Nagy in a conference call. "And I wanted my dream to come true and to fulfill my dream, and this was an opportunity to jump on board and get to the NFL as soon as possible, and the outcome is great. I believe I went to a great team, great organization, great coaches, just great overall everything, and I believe it worked out unbelievably."

"I knew one of their needs was tight end, and I believe it's a great fit, a great team," Gronkowski continued. "I believe I fit well in the organization. I'm just really happy."[xxx]

The Patriots needed to fill a gaping hole at the tight end spot. They recently released veteran Ben Watson, who finished second on the team in 2009 with five touchdown receptions. Before drafting Gronkowski, the only tight end on their active roster was Alge Crumpler. To further bolster New England's tight end depth, the team selected Florida Gators standout Aaron

Hernandez in the fourth round of the 2010 NFL draft at 113th overall.

Nagy believed Gronkowski would have been a first-round draft choice had it not been for the back injury which sidelined him for a year. The new Patriots tight end said that his back was in great shape at the time the team drafted him.

Gronkowski also could not contain his excitement at the thought of playing with three-time Super Bowl-winning quarterback Tom Brady.

"Catching passes from Tom Brady is going to be great," Gronkowski told Nagy. "He's one of the best quarterbacks to ever play the game. It's just going to be pretty cool."

He had another reason to be excited: the Dallas Cowboys recently signed his brother Chris as an undrafted free agent. Dallas was thinking of choosing him in the sixth or seventh round. However, that did not materialize in the end.

Not too many NFL teams draft fullbacks. Only three squads selected one in 2009. This reality did not surprise Chris Gronkowski at all. Despite being passed up, he still received an offer from the Cowboys mere minutes after the 2010 NFL draft ended.

Aside from the Dallas Cowboys, the St. Louis Rams (now the Los Angeles Rams), Kansas City Chiefs, and Carolina Panthers seriously considered Chris Gronkowski.

Rob Gronkowski finally realized another dream, which was for him to play with his brothers Dan and Chris in the National Football League at the same time. When Rob and Chris signed with the Patriots and Cowboys, respectively, Dan Gronkowski was already a Detroit Lions tight end.

Their head football coach at Williamsville North High School, Mike Mammoliti, could not have been prouder.

"It's just been a privilege for me and my staff," Mammoliti told the *Amherst Bee*. "It's an honor to have three guys out of the same high school, let alone the same family, play in the NFL. I think that might be a first in Western New York."

For his part, Rob Gronkowski signed his rookie deal with the New England Patriots on July 25, 2010. The four-year contract was worth $4.44 million with $2.59 million in guaranteed money and a $1.76 million signing bonus. He could also earn an additional $830,000 as a one-time incentive based on playing time.[xxxi]

Gronkowski was set to earn $320,000 in 2010, $405,000 in 2011, $490,000 (plus a $30,000 workout bonus) in 2012, and $575,000 (plus a workout bonus of $30,000) in 2013. He would become an unrestricted free agent in 2014.

2010 Preseason and Regular Season

During his two-year stint at the University of Arizona, Rob Gronkowski was one of the most decorated tight ends in college football. His back injury had forced him to sit out the entire 2009 NCAA football season. After the New England Patriots had drafted him in April 2010, Gronkowski was excited to take the field again, and one cannot blame him. If people consider that he got his first taste of NFL football in August 2010, that meant he was out of action for almost a year.

It did not matter.

Gronkowski was still the same force he was coming out of college. He was one of just three NFL players who scored four touchdowns in the 2010 preseason. The others were New York Giants wide receiver Victor Cruz and San Francisco 49ers running back Anthony Dixon.

It set the stage for Gronkowski's first NFL regular-season game at Gillette Stadium in Foxborough, Massachusetts, on

September 12, 2010. He figured to be instrumental in New England's continued dominance in the AFC. Since 2001, the Patriots have captured three Super Bowl titles and seven AFC East championships. They were seeking to win their first Vince Lombardi Trophy since 2004. However, the Baltimore Ravens beat them easily, 33-14, in the 2009 Wild Card Round.[xxxii]

Gronkowski's first regular-season game was against the Cincinnati Bengals. New England held a commanding 24-3 lead at the half. However, Bengals quarterback Carson Palmer spearheaded a mini-comeback to narrow the gap, 31-17, at the end of three quarters.

Patriots signal caller Tom Brady engineered a 14-play, 81-yard drive which ended with a one-yard touchdown pass to Gronkowski to make it 38-17 after the point after touchdown (PAT). Gronkowski handed the ball over to Brady before he took his blocking position for the extra point. The Bengals would get no closer than 14 points afterward.[xxxiii]

Gronkowski scored his first NFL touchdown in his very first regular-season game. But bigger things were yet to come for the product of Amherst, N.Y.

That moment came in a Week 10 showdown against the Pittsburgh Steelers on November 15, 2010. Gronkowski caught three touchdown passes in a 39-26 road win. He became the first rookie in franchise history and the youngest in league history to do so. Gronkowski was 21 years and 184 days old at the time. He beat the previous record, set by Minnesota Vikings wide receiver Randy Moss (21 years, 286 days), in a 1998 game against the Dallas Cowboys.[xxxiv] Ironically, Gronkowski and Moss were teammates for just four weeks. The 2010 NFL season was Moss' fourth with the Patriots. New England was also his third team in his 13-year NFL career. The team traded him just two days after its 41-14 Week 4 win over the Miami Dolphins. The Minnesota Vikings re-acquired him for a 2011 third-round draft choice.

Gronkowski returned to the Buffalo, N.Y. area in Week 16. He caught for two touchdowns and 54 yards on four receptions in a 34-3 romp over the hapless Buffalo Bills. His first touchdown catch, which occurred early in the second quarter, helped the Patriots pull away with a score of 13-3. New England would score 21 more points. The Patriots' defense also stifled the Bills, holding them scoreless the rest of the way. Tom Brady had also thrown 319 consecutive passes up to that point without an interception, which was a new NFL record (Cleveland Browns quarterback Bernie Kosar held the previous record with 308 bridging the 1990 and 1991 NFL seasons). More importantly, the Patriots (13-2) locked in the number 1 playoff seed in the AFC.[xxxv]

At the conclusion of the regular season, Rob Gronkowski amassed 546 receiving yards and ten touchdowns on 59 receptions.[xxxvi] Since the American Football League (AFL) and National Football League (NFL) merged in 1966, he became the first rookie tight end to record ten touchdowns. It had taken all of 44 years before it happened again, but Gronkowski proved to be more than up to the task. The Patriots' rookie tight end was also an iron man – he did not miss a single game or practice once he donned a New England jersey.

2010 Postseason

The New England Patriots were riding high during Rob Gronkowski's rookie season. They clinched the number 1 seed in the AFC and were primed to win their fourth Super Bowl trophy. LaDainian Tomlinson and the New York Jets were their first hurdle in the 2010 Divisional Round.

For Gronkowski, winning a title in his first NFL season would have been sweet. However, it was not meant to be.

Second-year New York Jets quarterback Mark Sanchez – nicknamed "The Sanchize" – threw three touchdown passes to lead his team to a 28-21 victory. The Jets would move on to their second straight AFC Championship Game. Unfortunately, they lost to the Pittsburgh Steelers, 24-19.

Despite the loss, New York still played well in their win over New England. Rex Ryan's team sacked Patriots quarterback Tom Brady five times. The Jets had held a 14-3 halftime lead before Brady rallied his troops. He threw a two-yard touchdown pass to Alge Crumpler with 15 seconds left in the third quarter. Sammy Morris' two-point conversion inched New England to within three at 14-11.[xxxvii]

The Jets stymied the Patriots' momentum as they outscored them, 14-3, in the ensuing 15 minutes. New England scored on another touchdown with just 30 seconds left to make the score more respectable, but it was too little, too late.

Once again, Rob Gronkowski made a good account for himself. He led all New England receivers with 65 yards on four receptions. He finished his rookie year with another strong showing. It was certainly something he could build on for the 2011 NFL season.

2011 Regular Season

If Rob Gronkowski's rookie season was a pleasant surprise, his sophomore year in the pro ranks would catapult him into stardom.

Gronkowski played an integral role in Tom Brady's amazing quarterbacking display in the 38-24 Week 1 win over the Miami Dolphins on September 13, 2011. Brady and Co. were eager to shake off the disappointing playoff loss to the Jets in 2010.

Brady threw for a franchise-record 517 yards and four touchdowns in the win over Miami. Four of his receivers – including Gronkowski – would record at least 86 yards. Wide receiver Wes Welker led the way for New England's receiving corps with 160 yards and two touchdowns on eight receptions. Gronkowski would finish with 86 yards and a touchdown on six receptions. The Patriots' two tight end set was too much for the Dolphins. Gronkowski and fellow 2010 draftee Aaron Hernandez combined for 189 receiving yards.[xxxviii]

Gronkowski would go on a mini-tear in the next two games against the San Diego Chargers and Buffalo Bills. He amassed a combined 195 yards and four touchdowns on 15 receptions. While New England beat San Diego handily, 35-21, they would lose on the road to Buffalo, 34-31. Gronkowski became an integral part of the New England passing attack. He also became one of Brady's favorite targets.

Although Gronkowski went on a four-game stretch without scoring a touchdown, he ended the drought in a big way. He had 96 yards and two touchdowns on just four receptions in a 34-3 rout of the visiting Kansas City Chiefs. He recorded a new career-high 52-yard reception in New England's opening six-play, 85-yard drive, and caught Brady's pass in the middle of the field to run for 35 yards. Gronkowski did a somersault as he made his way to the right side of the end zone. He spiked the ball ferociously – just one of many in his career – as he scored.

"When I get the ball," Gronkowski told ESPN. "You just don't want to go down. You've got to try and do something with the ball. That's why you get it."[xxxix]

Gronkowski added another touchdown reception in the third quarter for good measure. At that point, he already equaled his total of ten from his rookie season. His total of 20 was also the most for a tight end with two years of NFL experience. The Patriots had a 7-3 win-loss record. With six games left to play, Gronkowski still had plenty of time to inflict more damage on opposing defenses.

Not only that, he continued to re-write the NFL record books.

Gronkowski scored four more touchdowns in the next two games. Three of those came at the expense of the Patriots' struggling rivals, the 0-12 Indianapolis Colts, on December 4, 2011. Gronkowski now raised his second-year touchdown reception total to 13. It tied him with the San Diego Chargers' Antonio Gates (2004) and the San Francisco 49ers' Vernon Davis (2009) for the most number of touchdown receptions by a tight end in a season.

Gronkowski thought he eclipsed the mark when he scored another touchdown for a 31-3 Patriots lead with 4:17 left in the third quarter. However, the officials ruled it a run play instead. Before the ruling, Gronkowski held onto the ball, intending to keep it as a souvenir.

"I wasn't thinking about whether it was a pass or a lateral," Gronkowski told ESPN after the game. "I'll take the rushing touchdown. It's the first of my whole career."[xl]

The goal made it 14 for Gronkowski's career – the most ever for a tight end in a single season.

Despite falling behind by as many as 28 points, Indianapolis battled back behind second-string quarterback Dan Orlovsky's career night (353 yards, two touchdowns), but fell short, 31-24. New England improved to 9-3 on the season.

But Gronkowski was not quite done.

He scored four more touchdowns in the Patriots' remaining games of the 2011 NFL season. Two of those came in a 49-21 home win over the Buffalo Bills on January 1, 2012. Gronkowski set a new single-season mark for tight ends with 1,327 receiving yards. Interestingly enough, New Orleans Saints tight end Jimmy Graham broke the same record with his 1,310 receiving yards for the season earlier the same day. However, Gronkowski would have the final say. Former San Diego Chargers tight end Kellen Winslow held the previous record for 31 years.

Gronkowski broke the record when he caught a 22-yard pass from Patriots backup quarterback Brian Hoyer with 1:30 remaining in the game. New England head coach Bill Belichick called for the play so Gronkowski could break the record. He also ran his touchdown total on the season to 18 (17 receiving touchdowns and one rushing touchdown). The 18 total touchdowns and 17 receiving touchdowns were new NFL records for a tight end.

"It was cool, unbelievable," Gronkowski said. "It says a lot about this team."[xli]

It also said a lot about Gronkowski's performance.

Fans voted him to be the AFC's starting tight end in the 2012 Pro Bowl. He garnered 936,886 votes – more than three times the votes for the number 2 tight end, his teammate, Aaron Hernandez. Gronkowski finished third in AFC voting behind New England players Tom Brady and Wes Welker. *The Associated Press* also named Gronkowski to its 2011 All-Pro Team. Gronkowski received 44.5 of the 50 allotted votes. The Saints' Jimmy Graham finished a distant second with 5.5 votes.[xlii]

With Gronkowski firmly entrenched as a weapon at the tight end position, the New England Patriots clinched the number 1 seed in the AFC yet again. Now, they could only hope that they would do a much better job in the postseason.

2011 Postseason

The 2010 NFL season ended on a sour note for the New England Patriots. They still remembered the sorry loss at the hands of the New York Jets. With Rob Gronkowski elevating his game to new heights, New England was on the hunt for their fourth Super Bowl title.

Tim Tebow and the Denver Broncos were waiting for them in the Divisional Round. It turned out Tebow-mania did not have a chance from the beginning.

The Patriots established the early commanding lead and never looked back in a 45-10 rout of the upstart Broncos. Denver pulled off a stunning win in the AFC Wild Card round a week earlier. Tebow threw an 80-yard touchdown pass to Demaryius Thomas on the first play of overtime to secure a 29-23 victory at home.

This time, Tebow was just 9-of-26 passing for a 34.6 percent completion rate against the Patriots. He finished with 136 yards with no touchdowns for a paltry passing rating of 52.7. The New England defense also sacked him five times.

Meanwhile, Gronkowski continued his historic tear.

Tom Brady and Co. made him their top weapon in their dismantling of the Broncos – he finished with 145 receiving yards and three touchdowns on ten receptions. Brady threw for 363 yards and six touchdowns for New England. The Patriots' offensive line did a remarkable job of opening up the passing lanes for him – the Broncos failed to sack him in this pivotal game. As a result, Brady destroyed Denver's secondary from all angles.

"We were playing complementary football, and it was awesome," Gronkowski told ESPN. "Obviously, you can't start off the game any better than that."[xliii]

Next up were the Baltimore Ravens in the 2011 AFC Championship Game. Gronkowski's troops would rely on some luck in this one.

With the Patriots ahead 23-20 and only 11 seconds left in the game, Ravens kicker Billy Cundiff's 32-yard field goal attempt sailed wide left. New England was going to Super Bowl XLVI in Indianapolis to face Eli Manning and the New York Giants.

The score was tied at 10-10 when New England got the opportunity to pad their lead heading into halftime. On third down with a little over three minutes left in the half, Gronkowski caught a pass from Brady at the Ravens' 18-yard line. However, officials ruled him out of bounds. Patriots kicker Stephen Gostkowski made a 35-yard field goal to give his team a 13-10 lead at the break.

Gostkowski made another field goal with 9:09 in the third quarter. Baltimore scored the next 10 points to take the lead, 20-16. Brady's one-yard run capped off an 11-play, 64-yard drive in the early moments of the fourth quarter. The Patriots led 23-20 after Gostkowski made the extra point. Each team's defense held strong until the waning moments when Cundiff missed the critical field-goal attempt.

Gronkowski went to the training room for a short while so team doctors could check on an issue with his left leg. It turned out it was a minor one, and he took the field again moments later. He finished the day with 87 yards on five receptions.

He still could not believe he was going to his first Super Bowl game. It was too surreal.

"It doesn't even feel right, especially with the veterans here," Gronkowski told ESPN. "I watched them go to the Super Bowl as I was growing up and now I'm part of it. It is an unreal moment."[xliv]

After a season where Robert James Gronkowski broke several NFL records, he now had a chance to punctuate his new legacy with a Super Bowl championship.

Super Bowl XLVI vs. New York Giants

It turns out that there was a chance Rob Gronkowski might not have been able to play in Super Bowl XLVI against the New York Giants.

The earlier issue he had with his left leg against the Baltimore Ravens in the 2011 AFC Championship Game was a high ankle sprain. Despite the setback, a league source told NBC Sports' Mike Florio on February 4, 2012, that Gronkowski would suit up in the Super Bowl. Gronkowski's agent, Drew Rosenhaus, told NBC SportsTalk that week that his client would not play in that game had it not been the Super Bowl.[xlv] One can now say that Rob Gronkowski did not want to miss his first title game at any cost.

He confirmed this to *The Arizona Republic's* Kent Somers on February 3, 2012.[xlvi]

"It's the Super Bowl," Gronkowski said. "If it was a regular-season game, it wouldn't matter. It's the biggest game in sports history every year."

According to ESPN Boston's Mike Reiss, Gronkowski played in 96 percent of the Patriots' offensive snaps in the 2011 NFL season. What is more is that New England ran 80 percent of its snaps with at least two tight ends on the field, Gronkowski being one of them.[xlvii]

Patriots offensive coordinator Bill O'Brien – who would leave the Patriots to take over the embattled Penn State Nittany program rocked by a child abuse scandal – told Reiss that he remained undaunted.

"We're moving forward with the thought that we'll be ready for anything," he said. "We have a lot of good, instinctive players that will be ready for any role we ask them to do, right up to game time, during the game. They're adjustable guys, flexible guys, so we feel really good about where we're at right now."

Gronkowski was not around during the Patriots' practice six days before the Super Bowl. Nonetheless, O'Brien told ESPN that it was still "a good practice" and that they had "a few things to clean up."

The big day finally came. The city of Indianapolis hosted Super Bowl XLVI at Lucas Oil Stadium on February 5, 2012. It was the city's first time to host the Super Bowl. It was also the Patriots' second time facing the Giants in the Super Bowl in the last four years.

Once again, Eli Manning proved to be the New England Patriots' biggest nemesis.

Manning had orchestrated a historic last-minute drive four years earlier in Super Bowl XLII, denying New England the first perfect season in NFL history since the 1972 Miami Dolphins. It was the same game which featured the near-impossible catch Giants wide receiver David Tyree made. New York was down 14-10 with 2:39 remaining in the match. Manning's pass to Tyree was worth 32 yards. The Giants quarterback connected with wide receiver Plaxico Burress from 13 yards out for the game-winning touchdown with 35 seconds left. New York won 17-14 and Manning won his first Super Bowl trophy and Super Bowl MVP Award.

Back then, Rob Gronkowski was an 18-year-old freshman at the University of Arizona. Would he be able to make a difference in Super Bowl XLVI?

He would not. Eli Manning and Co. would prove to be too much in the end.

The Giants and Patriots provided the fans with another memorable Super Bowl match-up. New York got on the board first after the officials whistled Patriots quarterback Tom Brady for intentional grounding in his end zone. That penalty awarded New York two points. Five-and-a-half minutes later, Manning threw his only touchdown pass of the game to wide receiver Victor Cruz in the red zone. Cruz, as expected, did his salsa dance after he scored. The Giants led 9-0 after kicker Lawrence Tynes added the extra point.

New England's defense tightened in the second quarter. It held the Giants scoreless during that 15-minute span. After Stephen Gostkowski had nailed a 29-yard field goal, Brady engineered a 14-play, 99-yard drive. It culminated in a four-yard touchdown reception by Danny Woodhead. New England led for the first time, 10-9 after Gostkowski nailed the PAT.

With Gronkowski still hobbling because of his high ankle sprain, fellow Patriots tight end Aaron Hernandez tried to pick up the slack. He hauled in Brady's pass from 12 yards out at the 11:25 mark of the third quarter to pad New England's lead further at 16-9. The Giants failed to reach the end zone in the quarter, but did get two field goals from Tynes to make the score 17-15 for New England at the end for 45 minutes of play.

For his part, Manning shone brightly in the fourth quarter against the Patriots yet again.

He started things off with a fantastic 38-yard pass to wide receiver Mario Manningham with 3:46 remaining. Manningham's catch was just as sensational. He beat the Patriots in double coverage along the left sideline near midfield. The duo struck again twelve seconds later. Manning connected with Manningham for a 16-yard gain to move the sticks to New England's 34-yard line. After Manningham had managed a two-yard gain on the next play, Manning took to the air again. On 2nd and eight at the Patriots' 32-yard line, he passed to wide receiver Hakeem Nicks for a 14-yard gain. Four plays later, Giants running back Ahmad Bradshaw went down the middle for a six-yard touchdown. Despite the failed two-point conversion, New York regained the lead at 21-17.

Only 57 seconds remained on the game clock. The Patriots had to move the ball 80 yards downfield to win the game. Unfortunately, the Giants batted down Brady's desperation Hail Mary Pass to the end zone as time wound down. He targeted Aaron Hernandez, who had to ward off three Giants defenders. Brady's pass fell incomplete. The Giants overcame another Patriots lead to win their second Vince Lombardi Trophy in the last four years. Eli Manning won his second Super Bowl MVP Award. He finished the game with 296 yards, one touchdown, and no interceptions.

After the game, Rob Gronkowski told ESPN's Mike Rodak that his high ankle sprain was not an issue.[xlviii] He finished with just 26 yards on two receptions.

"I was good," Gronkowski said. "I was 100 percent out there doing everything they asked me to do."

When Rodak asked him about Brady's last-second Hail Mary pass, he thought it was a close call.

"It was a jump ball play," Gronkowski quipped. "Aaron did a great job of getting the ball deflected. I almost had it, but almost isn't enough."

Brady commended Gronkowski for toughing it out.

"He played his butt off," Brady told ESPN. "He fought. He came out to our practice on Thursday, and it's hard to believe he could play the game with the way he was feeling. He really toughed it out."

Patriots wide receiver Deion Branch also admired Gronkowski's toughness.

"With the role he did play, I tilt my hat off to that kid; he's a tough guy. I promise you 75 percent of the players in the NFL wouldn't play today, and this guy toughed it out for his team, and I truly appreciate that guy."

Gronkowski downplayed the notion that he would be undergoing offseason ankle surgery. Instead, he told Rodak he would receive various forms of treatment to help it heal.

Four days after ESPN interviewed Gronkowski, Dr. George Theodore performed arthroscopic left ankle surgery on the Patriots tight end. A team source told *The Boston Globe's* Matt Pepin that Gronkowski had torn multiple ligaments.[xlix]

In another development, Boston's 98.5 The Sports Hub's "Toucher and Rich" radio program (via CBS Boston) obtained exclusive video of Gronkowski and Patriots left tackle Matt Light dancing shirtless at the team's post-Super Bowl XLVI party. They danced to the music of hip-hop group LMFAO. 98.5 The Sports Hub posted the video on its Facebook page.[l]

The radio station's Jon Wallach said that Gronkowski and Light did nothing wrong.

"You have the 50- and 60-year-olds that say no. Give them a break, it's a long season. They earned the right to cut loose; I see no problem with it at all. They earned the bender that they got on Sunday."

Apparently, Gronkowski is an expert at putting tough losses behind him.

In November 2015, Gronkowski told *The New York Daily News'* Justin Tasch that he did not want to dwell on the Patriots' Super Bowl XLVI loss to the Giants only days before the two teams squared off in the 2015 NFL season.[li]

"You never want to revisit those memories," he said. "But it's definitely in the past, and we've got a chance to prove ourselves now, this Sunday. They're a good team, and we've got to be ready."

2012 Regular Season

Rob Gronkowski's 2011 NFL season did not end quite the way he wanted it to. Losing to the New York Giants in Super Bowl XLVI and undergoing surgery on his left ankle could have dampened his spirit, but he remained upbeat.

Because he exceeded everyone's expectations in just his second year in the NFL, the New England Patriots rewarded him in a huge way.

Gronkowski agreed to a lucrative six-year, $53 million contract extension on June 8, 2012. According to ESPN, this was the biggest deal a tight end has agreed to in NFL history. Gronkowski's hefty paycheck includes $16.5 million in guaranteed money. The Patriots can also choose to exercise a $10 million option in 2015. If they do, they will extend Gronkowski's contract until 2019.[lii]

NFL.com's Albert Breer and Ian Rapoport reported the deal as worth $54 million. It also includes an $8 million signing bonus.[liii]

Gronkowski's agent, Drew Rosenhaus, thanked the Patriots organization for giving his client a once-in-a-lifetime opportunity.

"This is a rare deal," he said. "Thanks to Mr. (New England Patriots owner Robert) Kraft and Mr. Belichick."

For his part, Gordy Gronkowski, Sr. told ESPN that the turn of events is "a remarkable story." He also said he was confident his son would remain humble.

"He broke every record last year, and it's just a remarkable story," he told ESPN. "And you know, there in Arizona, we didn't know if he was going to play anymore when he had his back surgery (in college). And now it's a great story. He's out there now, and everything's well, and he's ripping it up."

"No, Rob is Rob," he continued. "He still to this day will wear jeans that he had in high school and shirts that he had in high school. We're not flashy people. And that's Rob all the way. The money, it's nice, don't get me wrong, but it will not change him. Rob will always be Rob the goofball."

Gronkowski got off to a modest start in the 2012 season. He caught for a combined 156 yards and two touchdowns on 14 receptions in the Patriots' first three games. However, New

England got off to a miserable 1-2 start. The Patriots beat the Tennessee Titans in the opener by 21 points before losing to the Arizona Cardinals and Baltimore Ravens. New England would go on to win two of their next three games to improve to 3-3. After catching two touchdown passes in the first two games of the season, Gronkowski went through a slump. He caught just one touchdown pass in the next four games.

His best game during that stretch was against the Buffalo Bills on September 30, 2012. He caught for 104 yards and had a touchdown on five receptions in a 52-28 blowout win. The Patriots were down 21-7 with 11:08 remaining in the third quarter. They responded with six straight touchdowns to finish off the Bills, a team they had beaten 17 times in their past 18 games. Gronkowski teamed up with quarterback Tom Brady for the third touchdown during that run. Brady threw a 28-yard pass to Gronkowski to give New England the lead for the first time at 27-21 in the opening moments of the fourth quarter. Brady finished with 340 passing yards and three touchdowns.[liv]

The Patriots also set a franchise record with 45 second-half points. It was good enough for the fourth-most in league history.

"You can't panic," Gronkowski told ESPN. "When you panic, nothing good happens from there. We just stuck to the game plan."

After the Patriots had lost to the Seattle Seahawks by one point in Week 6, they recaptured their deadly form. New England extended their winning streak to four games after they routed the Indianapolis Colts, 59-24, on November 18, 2012. Gronkowski also began to gain some momentum. He had caught for an incredible seven touchdowns during that four-game run. He had 137 receiving yards and two touchdowns against the Colts. It was Indianapolis rookie quarterback Andrew Luck's first time facing the Patriots.

Gronkowski suffered a broken forearm in the win over the Colts. A league source told ESPN's Adam Schefter that Gronkowski sustained the injury when he blocked for an extra point with 3:55 remaining in the game. X-rays confirmed the injury, and NFL.com (via ESPN) reported on November 19 that Gronkowski would sit out the next four to six weeks.[lv]

He underwent surgery the following day. Patriots head coach Bill Belichick gave the media an update and explained why Gronkowski played special teams at that juncture of the game.[lvi]

"I don't really have anything," Belichick said. "I know that our medical people are looking at all the players today when they come in, trying to assess their situation like we always do on Monday. I'll catch up with them as they've had a chance (to gather that information)."

"It's one of his roles and jobs at the game," he continued. "Whoever does it, it's very important."

Patriots quarterback Tom Brady told Boston's WEEI Sports Radio (via ESPN) the Gronkowski incident was unfortunate. He and his teammates would have to adjust to playing without the Pro Bowl tight end.

"I knew he had gotten injured," Brady told WEEI. "But he's such a great player. It sucks that he gets hurt, but it's part of this game. He's got to do his best to get back as soon as possible, and we've got to go out there and win some games without him."

And that is what the Patriots did, even without Gronkowski. They won four of their next five games. Only the San Francisco 49ers beat them during that five-week span (a 41-34 win at Gillette Stadium on December 16). Patriots tight end Aaron Hernandez – who also battled injuries in 2012 – filled in for

Gronkowski. He scored three touchdowns during New England's late-season playoff push.[lvii]

Gronkowski's timeline for his return was accurate. He came back in time for New England's regular-season finale against the Miami Dolphins on December 30. The Patriots led 21-0 at halftime. Brady threw a 23-yard touchdown pass to Gronkowski with 9:25 remaining to finish off the scoring. The final score was Patriots 28, Dolphins 0.

New England finished the regular season with a 12-4 record. The Patriots won their third AFC East title since they had drafted Rob Gronkowski 42nd overall in 2010. As the second seed in the AFC, they also earned a bye in the Wild Card round.

Gronkowski, who missed the previous five games, told ESPN that it felt good to be back. He added that his performance boded well for the upcoming postseason.[lviii]

"It felt good," he said. "I haven't gotten hit in a while. I got limited reps (but) you always want to get some reps before heading into the playoffs."

Gronkowski had to deal with several injuries and a Super Bowl loss to the New York Giants in the past year. He hoped he and his Patriots teammates would be able to represent the AFC in Super Bowl XLVII in New Orleans.

2012 Postseason

The New England Patriots' foes in the Divisional Round of the 2012 NFL postseason were the upstart Houston Texans. The latter beat the Cincinnati Bengals 19-13 in their AFC Wild Card game on January 5. New England had to deal with Houston's Arian Foster – the league's sixth-leading rusher. The Patriots also had to figure out a way to stymie second-year defensive end sensation J.J. Watt.

They would also have to get past the Texans without Rob Gronkowski.

Gronkowski re-injured his left forearm during the Patriots' second possession of the game. On 2nd and 11 at the New England 22-yard line, quarterback Tom Brady threw an incomplete pass to Gronkowski in deep right field. Texans defensive end Antonio Smith covered Gronkowski on the play.

A team source told NFL.com's Albert Breer (via NFL.com's Gregg Rosenthal) that Gronkowski would miss the rest of the 2012 NFL postseason and that the re-injured forearm would require surgery. New England head coach Bill Belichick told the media after the game against the Texans, which was a 41-28 win, that Gronkowski would not have suited up had the injury been too severe. His loss further decimated the Patriots' lineup: running back Danny Woodhead and defensive end Chandler Jones missed the game against the Texans due to a thumb and ankle injury, respectively.[lix]

Tom Brady, Shane Vereen, and Wes Welker were the big-time performers against the Texans in the absence of their three teammates. Brady completed 25 of 40 pass attempts for 344 yards, three touchdowns, and no interceptions. He also notched his 17th career postseason victory. His three touchdown passes increased his career postseason total to 41. Only the San Francisco 49ers' Joe Montana (45) and the Green Bay Packers' Brett Favre (44) had more.

Vereen was big both on the ground and in the air. He recorded one rushing touchdown and two receiving touchdowns. Welker caught for 131 yards on eight receptions. Aaron Hernandez became the primary target at tight end for the Patriots and finished with 85 yards on six receptions.

Patriots head coach Bill Belichick also recorded his 17th postseason win, which tied him for third all-time behind the

Dallas Cowboys' Tom Landry (20) and the Miami Dolphins' Don Shula (19).[ix]

New England advanced to the 2012 AFC Championship Game against the Baltimore Ravens. The latter advanced after it stunned the Denver Broncos, 38-35, in double overtime. Justin Tucker's 47-yard field goal carried Baltimore into the next round.

The Ravens proved to be too much for the Patriots. Baltimore quarterback Joe Flacco threw three touchdown passes in the 28-13 win at Gillette Stadium. Although Brady finished with 320 yards and a touchdown, he converted on just 29 of 54 pass attempts. He also had two interceptions. Dannell Ellerbe and Cary Williams each had one pick for the Ravens' secondary. Middle linebacker Ray Lewis recorded 14 tackles for Baltimore.

The Patriots' offense just could not get it going in the second half. After establishing a 13-7 halftime lead, New England failed to score in the last 30 minutes of the game. The Ravens went on to beat the San Francisco 49ers 34-31 in Super Bowl XLVII.

For their part, the Patriots' Super Bowl title drought grew longer. They had not won the Vince Lombardi for the ninth consecutive season.

New England head coach Bill Belichick aptly summed up the loss to the Ravens.

"I'd probably say we came up a little short in every area," he said.[lxi]

For a second straight year, Rob Gronkowski's season did not end the way he wanted it to. His nagging forearm injuries forced him to miss several critical games, and as a result, his regular-season numbers went down. In 2011, he caught 17 touchdown passes. Despite missing five games, he still managed to record 11 touchdown receptions in 2012. Not too many tight ends could have done what he did.

Had he been healthy, it would have been a safe bet that the New England Patriots would have advanced deeper in the postseason. Who knows? They could have won Super Bowl XLVII.

Gronkowski could only hope he and the Patriots would make significant progress in the 2013 NFL season.

2013 Regular Season

Rob Gronkowski continued to experience issues with his left forearm weeks after the 2012 NFL season ended.

Gronkowski underwent a third surgery on his forearm in February 2013. According to ESPN, he went through the procedure because the forearm became infected. Because his doctors detected the infection early enough, he was expected not to miss a significant number of games in 2013, and they expected Gronkowski to be ready once training camp opened in late July.[lxii]

Many people criticized him earlier in the month after they saw a video of him doing a wrestling move on a friend at a Las Vegas nightclub. They thought it was inappropriate because his forearm was still in a fragile state.

Patriots offensive lineman Logan Mankins gave little importance to the incident. He said he did not have issues with Gronkowski "having fun."

On April 8, two team sources told ESPN Boston's Mike Reiss that Gronkowski would "very likely" undergo a fourth forearm surgery. Doctors would remove a plate in the forearm to make sure there that there would be no more remnants of the infection. He was expected to recover fully after ten weeks. Should the recovery period take that long, Gronkowski could miss a few games. On the other hand, the sources also said doctors could opt not to remove the plate.[lxiii]

Gronkowski discovered that his left arm was swelled and had some discharge during a trip to California. He contacted the

Patriots to inform them about the situation, and they immediately flew him back to Massachusetts to prevent the situation from worsening.

Gronkowski's agent, Drew Rosenhaus, told Miami television station WSVN-7 (via ESPN Boston) that he and his client would employ a wait-and-see approach.

"I can tell you that I'm gonna be talking to the team doctors," Rosenhaus said. "We're gonna talk to the experts, and we're gonna see how it plays out. Right now we've got plenty of time until the season starts, whether he needs another operation, what that operation will entail, that's very preliminary, that type of speculation is way off, no determinations have been made, there's no surgery scheduled, and we're not even sure if he's gonna need one."

Less than two weeks before Gronkowski's left arm swelled, he said it was in excellent shape in a morning interview on ESPN's "Mike & Mike in the Morning."

"I'm doing a lot better, definitely. Feeling a lot better," Gronkowski said. "My arm is feeling way better than it did during the playoffs and regular season when I broke it."

The hosts, Mike Greenberg and Mike Golic, then asked Gronkowski what he had been doing to treat his forearm.

"Right now, just rehabbing, getting the muscle stronger around it," he said. "You want to get everything activated, reactivated, because it shuts down for a little bit when it's healing. Just rehabbing, and when my trainers give me the 'good to go,' hopefully in the next couple (of) weeks, hopefully as soon as possible...I can get rolling again and get back in the weight room and get back on the field and do what I love doing – running around and catching some balls."

Gronkowski underwent a fourth surgery on his forearm on May 21. Surgeons installed new plates. They believed the infection which struck in early April had healed. Gronkowski was scheduled to consult his surgeon dating back to his Arizona Wildcat days, Dr. Robert Watkins, in three to four weeks. According to ESPN NFL Insider Adam Schefter, the Patriots tight end wanted to seek Dr. Watkins' advice if back surgery would have been necessary.[lxiv]

USA Today Sports' Mike Garafolo reported on June 19 that Gronkowski underwent successful back surgery. A source told Garafolo that the New England tight end was set for a late August return after he completed rehabilitation.[lxv]

It turned out that it would take a bit longer before Gronkowski could take the field again.

Exactly four months after Rob Gronkowski underwent a second back surgery, doctors cleared him to return to action. His agent, Drew Rosenhaus, confirmed this in an email to *USA Today Sports'* Tom Pelissero on October 18. The Patriots expected orthopedist Dr. James Andrews to clear Gronkowski a week earlier for the game against the New Orleans Saints. Instead, Gronkowski would play against New England's AFC East rivals, the New York Jets, on October 20. At the time Dr. Andrews cleared Gronkowski, the Patriots had a 5-1 win-loss record.[lxvi]

The big day finally arrived. Gronkowski showed no lingering effects of the nine-month layoff. Before the Jets game, he last took the field in the 2012 AFC Divisional Round playoff game against the Houston Texans. In this Week 7 showdown against the archrival Jets, Gronkowski was in top form. He finished with 114 receiving yards on eight receptions in the 30-27 overtime road loss. Jets kicker Nick Folk made the game-winning field goal with 5:07 remaining in the extra session.[lxvii]

Gronkowski could have won the game in regulation for New England. He ran a route toward the end zone and was about to catch the ball with one hand. However, he could not make the catch. The officials ruled the pass incomplete.

"I'm still mad about that one," Gronkowski told ESPN after the game.

Gronkowski caught a 16-yard pass from quarterback Tom Brady at the beginning of overtime. The Jets' defense prevented the Patriots from moving the sticks any farther. New England had to punt the ball, which set the stage for Folk's game-winning field goal.

Two weeks later, Gronkowski would have his biggest game of the season against the Pittsburgh Steelers.

Gronkowski caught one of Brady's four touchdown passes in the 55-31 win at Gillette Stadium. The former finished with 143 receiving yards on nine receptions for New England. Brady also threw for a season-high 432 passing yards – 252 in the first half. The Patriots held a 24-10 halftime lead and never looked back. They improved their record to 7-2.[lxviii]

Brady praised Gronkowski in an interview on the "Dennis and Callahan" show on Boston's WEEI sports radio (via ESPN).

"He's one of the best players in the NFL," Brady said. "We really haven't had him for a long time, and we've learned to play without him, but it's obvious when he's in there (that) he adds a different element to what we're trying to do, and that's why he's such a good player."

"He worked really hard to get back to his point," Brady added. "And after he's got a few games under him and he's got his football legs back hopefully he can continue to do it. It was a big spark for us yesterday, and he really came out making some big plays for us on third down, some drive starters when we got things going into the drive."

Brady paid Gronkowski more compliments in an ESPN interview.

"When (Gronkowski's) healthy and on the field, he's tough to stop," he said. "It's been a process for us, but at the bye week, 7-2 is not bad and, hopefully, our best football's ahead of us."

For his part, Gronkowski told ESPN that he had been feeling better.

"It felt great out there," he said. "It was important for us to play this way. Until now, we hadn't been clicking for all four quarters."

Gronkowski would come up with another impressive performance in New England's 34-31 road win over the

Houston Texans in Week 13. He had 127 receiving yards and a touchdown on 12 receptions. The Patriots improved to 9-3 while the Texans lost their 10th straight game. Houston's win-loss record dropped to 2-10.

Gronkowski's injury-plagued 2013 season would come to a premature end on December 9.

He suffered a suspected torn ACL in his right knee after Cleveland Browns safety T.J. Ward hit him in the third quarter of the Patriots' thrilling 27-26 win. The hit occurred after Gronkowski caught a 21-yard pass from Brady. He was set to undergo an MRI the following day. Before Gronkowski's latest injury, he had season totals of 560 receiving yards and 37 receptions – the most for tight ends.[lxix]

"If I would have hit him up high, there's a chance I would get fined and all that other stuff," Ward told ESPN. "So, I'm just being safe. It's kind of being caught between a rock and a hard place."

Ward also told reporters that he never meant to harm Gronkowski.[lxx]

"My intention is never to hurt anyone," Ward said. "That's not what this game is about. That's not how I play. I hate to see guys go down with any type of injury, and I just wanted him to know, whether he accepted it or not, it wasn't an intentional hit to injure him. But we have to play this game; we have to play it the way that they force us to, and unfortunately, we incurred an injury for him."

The Patriots fought back from a 19-3 deficit at home. Brady threw touchdown passes to Julian Edelman and Danny Amendola in a span of 61 seconds late in the fourth quarter to secure the win. New England improved its win-loss record to 10-3. The team also held on to the number 2 seed in the AFC.

On December 10, NFL Media Insider Ian Rapoport confirmed that Gronkowski had suffered a torn ACL, a torn MCL, and a slight concussion. He was ruled out for the rest of the 2013 NFL season. The Patriots also placed him on their season-ending injured reserve list.[lxxi]

As a result, New England signed tight end D.J. Williams to add depth. The Patriots needed all the help they could get. They had already released Aaron Hernandez in June after police arrested him on suspicion of murdering semi-pro football player Odin Lloyd.[lxxii]

The Patriots had won 10 of their 13 games when they lost Gronkowski for the season. Head coach Bill Belichick remained unfazed.

"However that may be, it may change from game to game," he said. "Obviously, we, unfortunately, had to play without Rob for (six) games at the beginning of this season. We may be in that situation again. We dealt with that already this year."

New England dealt with Gronkowski's absence well after they won two of their last three games to finish the regular season at 12-4. The Patriots locked up a fifth consecutive AFC East title in the process and also secured the AFC's number 2 playoff seed behind the Denver Broncos. As a result, New England drew a bye in the Wild Card round.

The Patriots met their rivals, the Indianapolis Colts, in the Divisional Round. They beat the Colts easily at home, 43-22. However, they lost in the 2013 AFC Championship Game to the Broncos on the road, 26-16.

The Seattle Seahawks would eventually win their first title in a 43-8 rout of Denver in Super Bowl XLVIII at MetLife Stadium in New Jersey.

Gronkowski suited up in just seven games for the Patriots in the 2013 NFL season because of injuries. He recorded a career-low 39 receptions and four touchdowns.

His season had ended in disappointment yet again. Nonetheless, his patience would pay enormous dividends the following year.

2014 Regular Season

Just before the New England Patriots 2013 postseason began, Rob Gronkowski underwent surgery on his torn right ACL. Dr. James Andrews performed the operation in Florida. According to ESPN Boston's Mike Reiss, Gronkowski's camp decided to delay ACL surgery for a month to allow the MCL to heal.[lxxiii]

After Gronkowski had sustained the injuries against the Cleveland Browns in early December 2013, he had been hanging out with his Patriots teammates. Reiss said that he and his teammates watched the movie "Lone Survivor" before their game against the Baltimore Ravens on December 20. Gronkowski watched the film in a wheelchair.

Almost five months later, Gronkowski told NESN's Doug Kyed at a Patriots Play 60 event at a grade school in Foxborough, MA that his rehabilitation was coming along just fine and that he was doing some offseason training on his own. He did not take part in the Patriots' first day of organized team activities (OTA) that week.[lxxiv]

"Just doing my own thing, just getting healthy on the side," Gronkowski said. "It's way different stuff. This year, basically just gotta be patient and just work hard and literally just give it all I can every single day. Right after this Play 60 event, I'll be going right to the building and go work out with my teammates, go through the rehab, go study up and everything. All I can ask for is to work hard every day and let the body heal and do what it does, and hopefully, when it comes down to it, I'm ready to roll."

Patriots owner Robert Kraft also told Kyed that he had seen Gronkowski working hard in the team's training room. The weekend before the Patriots Play 60 event, Gronkowski partied with Cleveland Browns rookie quarterback Johnny Manziel in Las Vegas.

Kraft downplayed this accordingly.

"He's just such a well-intentioned guy," he said. "He's a lot of fun, and I've never seen Gronk, in all the time with us, ever say or do anything that had a negative overtone. He's always out there. When you're building a team atmosphere with people with different backgrounds and different places, and it's a physical game, having someone like Gronk in the system is uplifting, especially if he's on the field all the time."

Finally, the good news came on July 23.

Patriots head coach Bill Belichick told the media at the start of training camp that Gronkowski's doctors had cleared him to play. Several of his teammates were very pleased with the development. One of them was defensive lineman Rob Ninkovich.[lxxv]

"Gronk is Gronk," he told CBS Boston. "Yo soy fiesta, right? He's a tremendous player, and personality-wise, he's one of the best guys you can meet...I'm happy to see his progress and happy to see him coming into this season."

Gronkowski's first regular-season game back from ACL surgery was on September 7 against the Miami Dolphins. He started the season the same way he had a year ago – returning after a nine-month layoff. He could have only hoped it did not hamper his play on the field.

Gronkowski played well in his return. It was not as great as some of his past performances, but it was a decent start. He had 40 receiving yards and a touchdown on four receptions in the Patriots' 33-20 Week 1 road loss. New England had a 20-10 lead at halftime. However, Miami's defense stifled the Patriots the rest of the way, not allowing them to score in the second half.[lxxvi]

It was the first time the Patriots lost a season opener in 11 years. Moreover, it was their first time they surrendered at least 23 points in the second half. The last time it happened was against the Pittsburgh Steelers on November 30, 2008. That covers a span of 94 games.

Dolphins running back Knowshon Moreno made the difference in this match. He finished with 134 rushing yards and a touchdown and ran for 91 yards in the second half. New England could only muster a total of 28 rushing yards in the last 30 minutes.

"They just played better," Gronkowski quipped.

New England got off to another slow start. The team went just 2-2 in their first four games. Gronkowski put up decent numbers with 147 receiving yards and three touchdowns during that stretch.

All of a sudden, the Patriots got hot.

They won seven straight games from early October until late November. During that time, they beat opponents by an average of 20 points. They beat perennial playoff contenders such as the Cincinnati Bengals (43-17 on October 5), Denver Broncos (43-21 on November 2), and Indianapolis Colts (42-20 on November 16) by an average margin of 23.3 points.

Gronkowski was a big part of that seven-game run. He averaged 95 receiving yards and recorded six touchdowns during that stretch. Any doubts about the torn ACL and past injuries dissipated.

Gronkowski's biggest game since he came off his ACL injury was against the Chicago Bears on October 26. He hauled in three of quarterback Tom Brady's five touchdown throws in a 51-23 victory at Gillette Stadium. Gronkowski had a total of 149 receiving yards.[lxxvii]

Bears linebacker Shea McClellin expressed his admiration for Gronkowski's style of play after the game.

"He can run well," McClellin said. He had great hands. And when you put that with a quarterback like Tom Brady, he's going to be tough to defend for anyone."

The Patriots' 26-21 loss to the Green Bay Packers in Week 14 snapped their seven-game winning streak. They promptly regrouped and won their last three games.

Rob Gronkowski made NFL history once again in one of those wins.

He became the first tight end to record four seasons with at least ten touchdown receptions in the 23-14 road victory over the San Diego Chargers in Week 15. New England also won at least ten games for the 12th consecutive year.[lxxviii]

The Patriots finished the 2014 NFL season with a 13-3 win-loss record. They earned a sixth straight AFC East title on their way to another first-round playoff bye. New England secured the conference's number 1 seed after the Cincinnati Bengals beat the Denver Broncos in Week 14.

Rob Gronkowski was in top form during the 2014 NFL season. He brought back memories of his memorable sophomore year in the pro ranks when he broke several league records for tight ends. He suited up in 15 games in 2014 – the most since 2011. His 1,124 receiving yards represented the second-most of his NFL career. He also scored 12 touchdowns – the second-highest total he has ever had.

He also made it to the Pro Bowl for the third time in his NFL career and also won the Comeback of the Year Award at the 2015 ESPYs.

Gronkowski could only hope he would carry this momentum into the 2014 NFL playoffs.

2014 Postseason

Robert James Gronkowski was now in his fifth NFL season and had already broken several league records. He also earned a hefty six-year, $53 million contract from the Patriots and even made it to Super Bowl XLVI against the New York Giants.

However, none of these things were enough. Gronkowski wanted to win the Super Bowl at all costs. At this point, it had been three years since he had made a significant impact in the playoffs. Now was his time to shine.

For the Patriots, the 2014 NFL postseason was a chance to reclaim lost glory. They last won the Super Bowl in 2004. Their fans wanted that drought to end. A rejuvenated Rob Gronkowski figured to be an instrumental part of this latest playoff run.

First up for the Patriots were the Baltimore Ravens – the very same team which beat them in the 2013 Divisional Round. New England was out for revenge.

In the previous year's playoff game, the Patriots blew a 13-7 halftime lead. They failed to score a point in the second half thanks in large part to Baltimore's dominant defense. Ravens quarterback Joe Flacco starred in the stirring come-from-behind 28-13 road win.

In 2014, it would be New England's turn to rally against Baltimore.

The Ravens opened up the scoring with two Flacco touchdown passes in the first quarter. The first one was a 19-yard throw to wide receiver Kamar Aiken in the game's opening drive. The second one was a nine-yard pass to Steve Smith, Sr. almost eight minutes later to put Baltimore up 14-0. It seemed that the Ravens had the Patriots' number once again. However, it was way too early. Brady and Co. had seen worse.

Brady took matters into his own hands. He ran the ball into the end zone in the waning moments of the first quarter to put New England on the board. After the Patriots' defense had held the Ravens to a three-and-out situation, the home team capitalized. On 2nd-and-10 at Baltimore's 15-yard line, Brady threw his second touchdown pass of the game, which found its way to wide receiver Danny Amendola to tie things up at 14 apiece.

After the Patriots had forced the Ravens to punt again, Brady threw an interception to Ravens linebacker Daryl Smith on New England's 35-yard line. Six plays later, Flacco recorded his third touchdown of the half when he connected with tight end Owen Daniels. Baltimore reclaimed the lead at the half, 21-14.

The Ravens increased their lead to 14 once again early in the third quarter. Flacco, who earned Super Bowl XLVII honors the previous season, showed everyone why he was one of the league's best quarterbacks. He threw a 16-yard pass to running back Justin Forsett to make it 28-14 after the extra point.

Gronkowski would strike back for New England in its next series.

Brady and his troops marched the ball downfield all the way to the Ravens' five-yard line. On 2nd-and-Goal, he threw a short pass to Gronkowski that ended in a touchdown. New England had trimmed the deficit to 28-21.

The Patriots held the Ravens to another three-and-out situation on the ensuing possession. It took New England just three plays to make Baltimore pay.

The Patriots then ran a trick play which resulted in wide receiver Julian Edelman – a quarterback in high school and college – passing the ball 51 yards downfield to Danny Amendola. It was another touchdown, which left the score at Patriots 28, Ravens 28.

Baltimore reclaimed the lead on Justin Tucker's 25-yard field goal early in the fourth quarter. Brady then threw his third and most decisive touchdown pass of the game to wide receiver Brandon LaFell with 5:13 remaining. Nine plays later, Flacco threw an interception intended for Torrey Smith. It was Patriots safety Duron Harmon who picked Flacco off. Brady took quarterback knees on the ensuing possession to secure the 35-31 win.

Gronkowski caught for 108 yards and a touchdown on seven receptions. It was his biggest playoff moment since he caught for 145 yards and three touchdowns against the Denver Broncos in the 2011 Divisional Round. He may have suffered several injuries in the past months, but his latest performance proved to everyone that he was back to his old self.

Next up for New England in the 2014 AFC Championship Game was a familiar foe: The Indianapolis Colts. The Patriots had several memorable playoff battles against the Colts which dated back to the Peyton Manning era, though this would be the first time they would face Andrew Luck in the postseason. Fans expected an exciting contest between the two teams.

It turned out to be a one-sided affair for the Patriots.

Behind 145 rushing yards and three touchdowns from LeGarrette Blount, New England cruised to a 45-7 rout of the visiting Colts. Quarterback Tom Brady converted on 23 of 35 pass attempts for 226 yards, three touchdowns, and one interception. Luck could only convert on 12 of 33 pass attempts for 126 yards, zero touchdowns, and two interceptions. The Patriots outgained the Colts on the ground, 177 yards to 83 yards. New England also enjoyed a huge discrepancy in the air. They had 226 receiving yards compared to Indianapolis' 126 yards.

Gronkowski did not record a breakout game. He caught for 28 yards a touchdown on three receptions.

The Patriots' win over the Colts had historical implications.

Tom Brady overtook John Elway as the quarterback with the most number of Super Bowl appearances (six). On the other hand, Bill Belichick tied Don Shula for most number of Super Bowl appearances (six). The Patriots also secured their all-time league best eighth Super Bowl visit. It moved them into a tie with the Dallas Cowboys and Pittsburgh Steelers.[lxxix]

The game would also be historical on a different scale. Fans will forever remember it as the infamous "DeflateGate" controversy. Brady allegedly conspired with two Patriots locker room attendants in deflating game balls for the 2014 AFC Championship Game. On May 11, NFL commissioner Roger Goodell suspended Brady for four games in the 2015 NFL season for his involvement. U.S. District Judge Richard Berman overturned the suspension on September 3, 2015.[lxxx]

Nonetheless, Rob Gronkowski was now in a position to make some history of his own. He could earn his very first Super Bowl ring.

Super Bowl XLIX vs. Seattle Seahawks

After four long years, Rob Gronkowski's health finally held up. It came at an excellent time; his New England Patriots were in a position to win their fourth Super Bowl title.

On Super Bowl XLIX Media Day, which was January 27, 2015, Gronkowski told reporters how great it felt to be healthy.[lxxxi]

"It feels good to be 100 percent healthy," he said. "And not get a million questions last time about my ankle."

He also said playing physical against the Seattle Seahawks – the NFL's top-rated defense – motivated him.

"It gets you amped up," he quipped. "That's what so special about (football) is how hard you can go and just take whatever you have built up and just go full speed at someone and level them. And someone can do that to you, so you've got to be ready at all times."

ESPN Boston's Jackie MacMullan reported three days before Super Bowl XLIX that running back Stevan Ridley and wide receiver Wes Welker had "long conversations" with Gronkowski, which kept his spirits up during the months he was inactive. Gronkowski's mother, Diane, could not contain her emotions when her son tore his ACL and MCL against the Cleveland Browns in December 2013. She promptly left her seat at Gillette Stadium and joined her son in the Patriots locker room.[lxxxii]

Gronkowski was already at full strength when the ESPN Boston report came out. He told MacMullan that winning a Super Bowl title would be one of his biggest accomplishments.

"This game's huge," Gronkowski said. "Legacies are based on this game for a lot of players – for Tom, for (former Patriots nose tackle) Vince (Wilfork), for the whole organization, and I feel, for the legacy of myself."

"(Winning) a Super Bowl is a lot different than being MVP or having an award for Outstanding Player. Being Super Bowl champion, I feel like if that occurs, it will no doubt be one of the greatest things that's ever happened (to me)."

Super Bowl XLIX took place on February 1, 2015, at the University of Phoenix Stadium in Glendale, Arizona.

It turned out to be one of the most exciting Super Bowl games of all time.

After a scoreless first quarter, the Patriots scored on their first drive of the second quarter. Tom Brady's 11-yard touchdown pass to Brandon LaFell made it 7-0 for New England. Seattle quarterback Russell Wilson was out to prove his worth in this one. The Seahawks selected him 75th overall in the 2012 NFL draft. Many draft experts believed that he plummeted that low because of his height (5'11"). He proved the naysayers wrong by leading his team to two consecutive Super Bowls. The Seahawks had won their first Vince Lombardi Trophy the year before. They blew out the Denver Broncos 43-8 in Super Bowl XLVIII.

After the Patriots and Seahawks had gone on consecutive three-and-out plays, Wilson engineered an eight-play, 70-yard drive. Running back Marshawn "Beast Mode" Lynch ended that drive with a three-yard touchdown run to tie things up after the extra point.

It did not take too long for New England to come right back.

Just over a minute later, Brady teamed up with Gronkowski for a 22-yard touchdown to give the Patriots the lead once again. Wilson proved that he was an elite quarterback when he led a five-play, 80-yard drive. He threw an 11-yard touchdown pass to Seahawks wide receiver Chris Matthews to tie the score at 14-14 at the end of the first quarter.

Super Bowl XLIX was living up to its billing.

The third quarter was all Seattle. Kicker Steven Hauschka made a 27-yard field goal at the 11:09 mark. Wilson threw his second touchdown pass of the game six minutes later to wide receiver Doug Wilson. Seattle was up 24-14 after 45 minutes.

The next eight minutes of play were a defensive struggle. Three of the next four drives were three-and-outs. When the Patriots regained possession, Brady and Co. decided that they had enough. The New England quarterback – a two-time Super Bowl MVP – showed why he is one of the game's best. On 3rd-and-14 at New England's 28-yard line, he found wide receiver Julian Edelman for a 21-yard gain. Brady then passed to Shane Vereen for a nine-yard gain. The officials also called Seahawks free safety Earl Thomas for unnecessary roughness on Vereen. As a result, the officials spotted the ball on Seattle's 27-yard line – a 15-yard penalty.

The Seattle defense forced New England to a 3rd-and-8 situation at the former's 25-yard line. Brady calmly passed to Edelman for a critical 21-yard gain for first down. Two plays later, Brady connected with Danny Amendola for a touchdown.

The Patriots' defense forced the Seahawks to punt after just three plays. Brady and Co. made them pay. Ten plays and 64 yards later, Brady found Edelman in the end zone to put the score at Patriots 28, Seahawks 24. The New England quarterback finished with 328 yards, four touchdowns, and two interceptions. He kept the vaunted Seattle secondary, known as the "Legion of Boom," guessing all game long. All four of his touchdown passes were to different receivers (Edelman, Gronkowski, Amendola, and LaFell). Brady became the leading touchdown passer in Super Bowl history, eclipsing Joe Montana's previous record of 11.[lxxxiii]

Brady's fourth touchdown pass not only gave New England the lead, but it also set the stage for one of the wildest Super Bowl finishes ever.

On Seattle's next series, Wilson passed deep left to Lynch for a 31-yard gain all the way to New England's 49-yard line. When play resumed after the two-minute warning, Wilson threw two incomplete passes. The Seahawks faced a 3rd-and-10 situation in the Super Bowl and had to convert at all costs.

Wilson remained composed. He threw an 11-yard pass to Ricardo Lockette for first down. The Seattle quarterback heaved a pass to the deep right that was intended for wide receiver Jermaine Kearse. The latter made an unbelievable catch at the Patriots' five-yard line with 1:14 remaining.

After the Seahawks had called timeout, Lynch rushed for four yards. Seattle now had a 2nd-and-goal situation at New England's one-yard line with 26 seconds left.

Fans and experts alike expected Wilson to hand the ball to Lynch in that kind of situation. Few running backs were more dangerous in the red zone than Lynch.

Instead, Wilson threw a short pass intended for Lockette. After the latter had hit the turf, the ball came loose. Patriots rookie cornerback Malcolm Butler stepped into the passing lane and recorded the interception – the very first of his NFL career.

Just when the Patriots were about to celebrate their fourth Super Bowl title, a skirmish broke out after Brady took a knee in the ensuing series. Players from both sides shoved one other, and Rob Gronkowski was in the middle of it all. He and Seahawks linebacker Bruce Irvin got into a heated shoving match. Irvin also got into it with New England tight end Michael Hoomanawanui. Officials ejected Irvin after the melee.

The NFL fined Irvin $10,000 and also slapped an $8,628 penalty on Gronkowski and Seahawks defensive end, Michael Bennett. Seattle wide receiver Doug Baldwin received an $11,025 fine for his unsportsmanlike conduct penalty in Super Bowl XLIX.[lxxxiv]

Despite the turn of events, Rob Gronkowski won his first Super Bowl title. He played a key role in securing New England's fourth Vince Lombardi Trophy and finished with 68 yards and a touchdown on six receptions. Tom Brady earned his third Super Bowl MVP honors.

Gronkowski poured out his emotions to the Patriots' official website after the win over the Seahawks.[lxxxv]

"This is an unbelievable feeling," Gronkowski said. "We played such a great team game together. What a great team victory. It's unbelievable. This is indescribable."

Just like he did after the Super Bowl XLVI loss to the New York Giants three years earlier, Rob Gronkowski partied. This time, he partied as a member of the winning team. According to

NESN's Ricky Doyle, he danced and took the stage with Patriots owner Robert Kraft and rappers Flo Rida and Rick Ross after New England's Super Bowl XLIX win.[lxxxvi]

Nobody could blame Gronkowski for really cherishing the moment.

2015 Regular Season

Rob Gronkowski finally enjoyed an injury-free offseason. Not only that, he was coming off his first Super Bowl win. Nothing could be better.

Gronkowski and his Patriots teammates received their Super Bowl rings at owner Robert Kraft's house on June 15, 2015. Once the awarding ceremonies concluded, Gronkowski, Kraft, Tom Brady, and the other Patriots danced and partied into the night.[lxxxvii]

The New England Patriots' goal for the 2015 NFL season was simple: repeat as Super Bowl champions. A healthy Rob Gronkowski was an integral part of that aspiration.

Gronkowski started the season on an encouraging note.

He caught three of Tom Brady's four touchdown passes in the 28-21 home opener against the Pittsburgh Steelers on September 10. Gronkowski caught two touchdowns in the first quarter to put New England up, 14-0, and caught his third touchdown pass in the fourth quarter to put away the game for good. Gronkowski recorded the third three-touchdown game of his six-year NFL career, which was good for second in franchise history. Former Patriots wide receiver Randy Moss holds the record with four.

The Steelers – who played without running back Le'Veon Bell and center Maurkice Pouncey – scored a meaningless touchdown with two seconds left to make the final score more respectable.

The Patriots unveiled their fourth Super Bowl title banner before the game. Brady, who felt relieved to play after Judge Richard M. Berman overturned his four-game suspension, spoke about Gronkowski's value.[lxxxviii]

"Anytime they don't cover Gronk, he usually gets it," Brady said.

Unlike the previous year, the Patriots got off to a fast start in 2015. They won their first ten games of the season. During that run, Gronkowski caught for 842 yards and eight touchdowns. He also caught for at least 101 yards in five games. New England won by an average margin of 15.8 points in those five games.

The law of averages then caught up with the Patriots.

The Denver Broncos beat the New England Patriots in overtime, 30-24, in a Week 12 showdown. The latter suffered its first loss of the 2015 NFL season. Broncos running back C.J. Anderson broke loose from the Patriots' defense for the decisive 48-yard touchdown run in the extra session.

Gronkowski put up respectable numbers – 88 yards and one touchdown on six receptions – in the defeat. New England lost not only the game, but also its Pro Bowl tight end in the waning moments of the match. Gronkowski suffered a knee injury after Denver safety Darian Stewart hit him with 2:49 remaining in the game. Officials ruled that it was a clean hit. The Patriots' staff carted Gronkowski off the Sports Authority Field at Mile High.[lxxxix]

The Patriots issued a statement on Gronkowski's latest injury two days later:[xc]

"During Sunday night's game, Rob Gronkowski sustained a bone bruise/sprain of his right knee. His status will be evaluated on a week-to-week basis and listed accordingly on the practice participation and injury reports. There is no timetable for his readiness to return, which will be determined in the days or hours prior to the appropriate game. Any timetable reported prior to that final determination would be speculative."

Gronkowski sat out the Patriots' 35-28 home loss to the Philadelphia Eagles in Week 13 where New England suffered its second straight defeat. Gronkowski returned for the following week's game against the Houston Texans.

Patriots quarterback Tom Brady threw a touchdown pass to Gronkowski on 1st-and-Goal just before halftime. New England went on to win on the road convincingly, 27-6. The Patriots clinched a playoff spot in the process.

Gronkowski, who finished with 87 yards and a touchdown on four receptions, told ESPN that he felt good after missing the game against the Eagles.[xci]

"It's always good to make a play, get a touchdown," he said. "The icing on the cake is that win."

Two weeks after Gronkowski injured his knee against the Broncos, he ran into another setback.

According to CBS Boston, his close family friend and trainer Dana Parenteau died on December 18. Gronkowski found out about it in the early morning hours and eventually missed practice that day. The two had known each other for five years and met during Gronkowski's rookie year in 2010.[xcii]

The New England Pro Bowl tight end dedicated the December 20 game against the Tennessee Titans to Parenteau. After he had scored a first-quarter touchdown, he raised his arms toward the sky.

"My good friend loved the game of football, loved being at all my games, always had my back, I definitely dedicated that touchdown to him," he said. "I pointed up, I know he was up there watching. Definitely, that score (a Patriots' 33-16 home win) was for him, and I know he was going crazy, knowing it was dedicated to him."

The Patriots finished the 2015 NFL season with a 2-2 record after Gronkowski returned. Despite the mediocre finish, they still finished with a 13-3 overall win-loss record, good enough for the number 2 seed in the AFC. Gronkowski caught for 245 yards and two touchdowns in those four games.

With a bye in the Wild Card Round, the Patriots were in a good position to defend their Super Bowl title.

2015 Postseason

First up for the New England Patriots in the 2015 Divisional Round were Jamaal Charles and the Kansas City Chiefs. The Chiefs had not made the AFC Championship Game since 1993, which was a 22-year drought. That year, Kansas City had lost to the Buffalo Bills. In 2015, the Chiefs wanted nothing less than their first Super Bowl title in the NFL. They had won Super Bowl IV in 1969 when they were still part of the American Football League (AFL) before the merger. Now they had to go through the defending champions.

Rob Gronkowski and Co. would thwart the Chiefs' lofty aspirations.

The Patriots' Pro Bowl tight end got things going early in the first quarter. He hauled in an eight-yard pass from Tom Brady to put New England up, 7-0. Kansas City would go on a 17-play drive which chewed eight minutes and 31 seconds off the game clock. Chiefs kicker Cairo Santos nailed a 34-yard field goal to make it 7-3.

The next 14 minutes were a defensive struggle. Four possessions ended in punts, and the Patriots and Chiefs traded three-and-outs in the last two drives.

It took New England five minutes and 31 seconds to reach the end zone once again. Brady ran the ball into the end zone on 3rd and Goal for a 14-3 lead. Santos made another field goal a little more than three minutes later. New England held an eight-point halftime lead.

Kansas City had possession to start the second half. The Chiefs managed to march the ball to New England's 40-yard line at the 10:31 mark. However, Kansas City running back Knile Davis fumbled the ball, and New England linebacker Chandler Jones recovered. The Patriots would make the Chiefs pay for the costly miscue.

It took New England just five plays to score another seven points. On 1st-and-10 at Kansas City's 16-yard line, Brady passed to Gronkowski. The latter found a seam in the left part of the field and took it all the way to end zone. The Patriots led 21-6 after the extra point.

Twelve plays later, Chiefs quarterback passed to wide receiver Albert Wilson for a 10-yard touchdown. New England would make field goals in two of the game's next three drives for a 27-13 lead. Kansas City scored a touchdown with 1:13 remaining. However, it was too little, too late.

Gronkowski was in top form. He finished with 83 yards and two touchdowns on seven receptions. His 16-yard touchdown early in the third quarter was the difference. The Chiefs were not able to overcome the deficit. Gronkowski also recovered a crucial onside kick in the fourth quarter to stymie Kansas City's rally.[xciii]

New England was moving on to the AFC Championship Game for a fifth straight year. To put things in perspective, the Patriots have made five AFC Championship Games and two Super Bowl games since they drafted Rob Gronkowski in 2010.

For the Patriots to successfully defend their crown, they had to beat a familiar nemesis: Peyton Manning.

The New England Patriots and Denver Broncos last met in the postseason in the 2013 AFC Championship Game. Manning's Broncos prevailed over a Gronkowski-less Patriots, 26-16. The Patriots were out for revenge. Brady had an 11-5 edge in his all-time games against Manning entering the 2015 AFC Championship Game. However, Manning had a 2-1 edge over Brady in AFC title games dating back to the former's days with the Indianapolis Colts.

Brady had his work cut out for him. He would face the Broncos' league-leading defense. Denver was one of just two teams – the Seattle Seahawks being the other – to limit their opponents to fewer than 300 yards per game in the regular season. The Broncos were also the only team to limit their opponents to fewer than 200 passing yards per game (199.6).[xciv]

On the other hand, the Patriots were the second-highest scoring team in the NFL (29.1 points per game) and also ranked sixth in total net yards.[xcv]

Something had to give.

The game took place at the Broncos' Sports Authority Field at Mile High on January 25, 2016. New England searched for their form in the early game. The Patriots uncharacteristically punted on their first three possessions. Denver defensive coordinator Wade Phillips had Brady and Co. on their heels.

For his part, Manning helped the Broncos move the ball methodically downfield. They started things off with an 11-play, 83-yard drive, which ended in Manning passing to tight end Owen Daniels for a 21-yard touchdown to put the score at Denver 7, New England 0.

As they did in the 2015 AFC Divisional Round against the Chiefs, the Patriots capitalized on their opponents' mistakes.

On 2nd and eight at Denver's 28-yard line and with 2:27 left in the first quarter, officials ruled Manning's pass to Ronnie Hillman as incomplete. Patriots head coach Bill Belichick challenged the ruling. The officials reversed it, saying it was fumble which New England linebacker Jonathan Freeny recovered. Two plays later, newly-acquired Patriots running back Steven Jackson ran the ball in for a one-yard touchdown. However, kicker Stephen Gostkowski's extra point attempt sailed wide right. It was no good.

And it proved to have critical repercussions in the endgame.

Brady also had problems with the Denver defense all game long. Early in the second quarter, New England spotted the ball on its 13-yard line. Brady threw a short pass that was intended for Gronkowski. However, Broncos linebacker Von Miller stepped in to intercept it. Less than a minute later, Manning found Daniels in the end zone again for a 14-6 Broncos lead. Both teams would then trade field goals to make it 17-9 for Denver at halftime.

The Broncos and Patriots' defenses were the dominant theme in the third quarter – the two teams combined for five punts during that 15-minute stretch. Gostkowski provided the only offense in the quarter when he made a field goal at the 10:26 mark. Denver's Brandon McManus would make a field goal of his own early in the fourth quarter to make it 20-12 for the Broncos.

That set up a wild finish.

New England got the ball with just 1:52 left to play. Brady and Co. spotted the ball at midfield after a Denver punt. Faced with a 4th-and-10 situation and the season on the line, Brady somehow found Gronkowski rushing up the middle for a 40-yard gain. The Broncos' Josh Bush and Chris Harris, Jr. tackled Gronkowski on Denver's 10-yard line. Brady connected with Julian Edelman for a six-yard gain on 2nd and Goal.

Two plays later, Brady threw to Gronkowski in double coverage for the touchdown. New England had to go for the two-point conversion to force overtime. Had Gostkowski made his earlier extra-point attempt – his first miss in 524 attempts – the Patriots would have gone for the extra point after Gronkowski's last-second touchdown.

Brady tried to pass to Edelman for the two-point conversion, but Broncos cornerback Bradley Roby intercepted it. The Denver Broncos were moving on to Super Bowl 50. The New England Patriots were going home.

After the game, Gronkowski refused to blame Gostkowski's missed extra-point attempt for the sorry loss.[xcvi]

"It's not just one individual's fault," he said. "You can't put it in the hands of Steph. There's no way."

Gronkowski – who finished with 144 yards and one touchdown on eight receptions – told the Patriots' official website that he had battled through cramps during the game against the Broncos due to the high altitude. He said that he drank a lot of water to counteract the effects.[xcvii]

Despite New England not being able to defend its Super Bowl title, Gronkowski told the team's official website he was still proud of his team.

"I'm proud of this team," he said. "The defense, you've got to give them credit. They did a great job today. Just throughout this whole season, throughout this whole game, you've got to be proud to be on this team. Everyone fought, everyone battled, and everyone gave it all they got. I'm proud to be part of this season. It was a great season overall, and it just came down to that two-point conversion. Like I said, Denver made more plays than us."

The New England Patriots' title quest did not succeed in the 2015 NFL season. Nonetheless, with a healthy Rob Gronkowski ready to go, the Patriots should be primed to win another Vince Lombardi Trophy in 2016.

2016 Regular Season

The 2016 season was going to be unlike anything the New England Patriots had experienced in franchise history. The first play was in a court of law in late April, as the Second Circuit of the United States Court of Appeals ruled in favor of NFL Commissioner Roger Goodell in that he had "broad discretion" as part of the Collective Bargaining Agreement with the NFLPA when it came to handing out discipline in the form of fines and suspensions.

The ruling overturned a lower-court decision in favor of Tom Brady and his successful appeal of his four-game suspension and brought about a final chapter to the "DeflateGate" saga, which had now gone on for 15 months due to Brady's decision to challenge his ban through the legal process. The result was that Brady would sit out the first four games of the 2016 season, creating many question marks for the perennial Super Bowl contenders.

The biggest question, who would play quarterback, actually had an easy answer. Jimmy Garoppolo, the team's second-round pick in 2014, was seen as an eventual successor to Brady in New England, though no one knew what sort of time frame for the actual passing of the torch would be. Brady has been adamant about playing quarterback well into his 40s, and his fanatical devotion to health and fitness has made him one of the most durable quarterbacks in NFL history, his freak torn ACL in the 2008 season opener notwithstanding.

If there was a silver lining to Brady's suspension, it was that Brady would be allowed to practice with the team during the preseason and be available to offer Garoppolo all the advice he needed as he got to work with the first team.

But lost in the daily drama of what was going on at the quarterback position, Gronkowski inadvertently created some of his own. He suffered a hamstring injury in mid-August,\ and it continued to bother him throughout the preseason. While there would be no definitive diagnosis on the severity of the injury, it got to a point before the season opener against Arizona that Gronkowski told NFL Media that he was "week-to-week" because of his ailing hamstring.

The Patriots, though, had bolstered their depth at tight end by acquiring Martellus Bennett from the Chicago Bears in March for a fourth-round pick in the 2016 draft. Bennett had been one of the primary playmakers for the Bears, catching a career-high 90 passes in 2014 and 53 the following season, but Chicago had started rebuilding in earnest. The Bears were a team in need of draft picks since they wanted to get younger and accelerate their timetable. In retrospect, the price of a fourth-round pick for a steady, capable veteran such as Bennett turned out to be a steal for New England.

Gronkowski was ruled out of the season opener at Arizona where the Cardinals were coming off one of their best seasons in franchise history at 13-3 and had been pegged as a potential Super Bowl contender.

Any nerves Garoppolo may have had in his first NFL start never showed as he completed 24 of 33 passes for 264 yards and a touchdown as New England opened the season with a 23-21 victory. He guided the Patriots on a 13-play, 61-yard drive that ended with Stephen Gostkowski booting a 32-yard field goal with 3:44 to play for the game's final points.

Gronkowski's availability was unknown ahead of New England's home opener against Miami in Week 2, but unfortunately, his hamstring again did not respond to treatment, and he was forced to watch from the sidelines. Garoppolo again looked like a seasoned veteran, completing 18 of 26 passes for 232 yards and three touchdowns, but he suffered a right shoulder injury in the 31-24 triumph.

The absence of Gronkowski coupled with Garoppolo's grasp of the offense resulted in a more balanced passing attack. Seven different players caught at least one pass in each of those first two games, but for Week 3, rookie and third-stringer Jacoby Brissett would be under center.

Brissett was a third-round pick from North Carolina State where he transferred to from Florida for the final two years of his collegiate career. He threw for 5,268 yards and 43 touchdowns in his two seasons with the Wolfpack, but here he was being thrown into his first NFL experience just two weeks into his first NFL season.

He did not have to do much in his mop-up role against Miami but performed well by completing 6 of 9 passes for 92 yards and led the Patriots on a scoring drive that turned out to be important given the final score. Now he was not only going to make his first professional start, but he was going to do it on a quick turnaround as the Patriots were hosting the Houston Texans on Thursday night.

Gronkowski was finally cleared to play, but there was no sense of how much he would be able to contribute or even what his role in the offense would be given how much it had been revamped from first Brady to Garoppolo and now to Brissett.

It turns out that the game plan was changed plenty. Not that it mattered much because the Patriots defense picked up Brissett with an impressive performance in a 27-0 rout of the Texans. New England forced three turnovers and Brissett played within the offense, completing 11 of 19 passes for 103 yards while also running for a 27-yard touchdown to give the Patriots a 10-0 lead late in the first quarter.

As for Gronkowski, he was used mainly as a decoy and a blocker. He logged a total of 14 snaps, and just three came in the second half. Of those 14 plays, 13 were running plays, and he admitted afterward to NESN that the one pass pattern he ran was full of rust.

"Oh yeah, that wasn't that good," he said with a laugh. "We're just going to throw that one out. I don't even know if I want to watch it. But it's all good. We got that win, baby."

The Thursday night game meant that the Patriots had some extra rest ahead of their Week 4 contest at home versus Buffalo to complete Brady's suspension. Brissett would again be under center, but Bills head coach Rex Ryan has always schemed well against opposing rookie quarterbacks, and this game would be no different.

Ryan also takes an astonishing amount of pleasure in matching wits against Belichick and the Patriots, and the 16-0 whitewashing was New England's first shutout defeat at Gillette Stadium and first at home since a 6-0 loss to the New York Jets in 1993.

Gronkowski was more involved in the offense in the sense he participated in more plays, but the results were not there. He was targeted only twice and finished with just one reception for 11 yards, partially due to the Bills' defense and partially due to the lack of cohesion with Brissett. That is neither players' fault; that is just the NFL reality of having a third-string rookie quarterback pressed into duty while a star tight end is working his way back to 100 percent health.

But all things considered, the Patriots were in good shape. They went 3-1 without their starting quarterback and most of those games without their best receiving option and held their customary spot atop the AFC East. Belichick and Co. could not have hand-picked a better opponent for Tom Brady to return for his season debut as New England was traveling to Cleveland to play the woeful Browns, who were 0-4 and had allowed 1,039 passing yards in those games.

And the highly motivated Brady never missed a beat in his return. He threw for 406 yards and three touchdowns as New England waxed Cleveland 33-13. Gronkowski did not catch any of those three scoring tosses, but he was a huge factor as he caught five passes for 109 yards. On the Patriots' first scoring drive, Gronkowski caught two passes for 53 yards, including a 34-yard reception to the Cleveland 2-yard line.

That second catch, coming on a 3rd-and-8, was vintage Gronkowski. He went over the middle from left to right on a crossing pattern, stepped out of one tackle, slipped out of a second, and rumbled down the right sideline before being gang-tackled just short of the goal line.

With the Patriots' offense finally having all its parts on the field, there was something eerily familiar about its ruthlessness. New England was going to use Bennett and Gronkowski similar to earlier in the decade when Gronkowski and Aaron Hernandez terrorized opposing secondaries by creating mismatches due to their size and speed in the middle of the field.

According to the MassLive blog, Bennett and Gronkowski were used as traditional tight ends together on 30 plays versus Cleveland. In the 11 passing plays called, Brady completed 7 of 10 passes for 105 yards, including a 37-yard touchdown toss to Bennett and a 37-yarder to Gronkowski that eventually led to a field goal.

The good times continued in Week 6 when Brady has his first home game of the season against the Cincinnati Bengals. Gronkowski finally found the end zone on a four-yard scoring toss that put New England ahead 19-14 and was part of a 25-point second half as the Patriots pulled away for a 35-17 victory.

Gronkowski finished with seven catches for a career-high 162 yards, with 121 of them coming in the second half. There was also a sighting of the fun-loving Gronkowski fans have come to know, as he did a disco dance to celebrate LeGarrette Blount's victory-sealing touchdown in the fourth quarter.

"Yeah that was a little disco dance," he told NESN. "But just a little celebration that we scored right at the end, LeGarrette did a great job. He just barely missed getting in on that first play, and then on the second one, he launched himself over and got that touchdown, so it was a little celebration, staying clear from any penalties."

Gronkowski did not let up the following week at Pittsburgh where New England won 27-16 to improve to 6-1 and asserted itself as one of the contenders in the AFC. He had four catches for 93 yards, and his 36-yard touchdown reception in the third quarter blunted a Steelers rally after they had closed within one point.

Gronkowski added a key 37-yard catch-and-run that contributed to a drive that ended in a Blount touchdown run that assured another victory. The touchdown was the 68th of his career, tying him with wide receiver Stanley Morgan for the most in Patriots history.

Next up for New England was a trip to Buffalo, where it had the chance to avenge its only loss of the season. Gronkowski would team up with Brady to make sure revenge would be a dish served cold in upstate New York as the Patriots ran roughshod on the Bills in a 41-25 victory.

Brady threw two first-quarter touchdown passes and finished with four overall, but it was his 53-yard hookup over the middle with Gronkowski in the second quarter that stuffed Buffalo's momentum after the Bills had closed within 14-10 and sent the Patriots on their way. It was also the 69th career TD for Gronkowski, giving him sole possession of the team's all-time mark. He celebrated with a bow in a place near and dear to his Amherst, New York, upbringing.

Gronkowski admitted the revenge victory felt nice, telling The Associated Press, "You know, they like to talk all that. They got that win. I'm so glad we came in here and showed them what we're really about."

New England went into the bye with a 7-1 mark, but the team and Gronkowski's fortunes would take a turn as it hosted Seattle on Sunday Night Football in Week 10. It was the first time the teams had met since Super Bowl XLIX, and it would again pit Gronkowski against one of the league's elite secondaries, the "Legion of Boom" that featured Kam Chancellor, Earl Thomas, and Richard Sherman.

It was an intense, physical contest. Gronkowski was forced to leave the game late in the second quarter after a thunderous hit to the chest by Thomas as he ran a seam route. He had gotten by Chancellor, who made a play to break up the pass before Thomas unloaded a clean shoulder-first hit. The blow left Gronkowski dazed, and he was eventually walked to the sideline for further evaluation.

Gronkowski, though, apparently passed the concussion protocol because he returned to the game. He nearly helped the Patriots force overtime, but he was unable to corral a pass in the end zone on 4th-and-1 with 14 seconds left after hand-fighting with Chancellor. The result was a 31-24 loss that dropped New England to 7-2, but the fallout from the hit was still yet to come.

Both Gronkowski and Thomas confirmed it was a clean hit, with Gronkowski saying post-game it was "probably one of the hardest I've been hit in my career, for sure, by a good player. A good, fast player who's like a missile." He added that Thomas "hit me fair and square. It's football. You're going to get laid out eventually."

But the impact of the blow reverberated throughout Gronkowski's body and affected more than his chest and sternum area. He suffered a perforated lung from the hit and did not fly with the team to San Francisco where they bounced back with a 30-17 victory over the 49ers.

Gronkowski returned the following week against the New York Jets, but he was forced to leave in the first quarter with what was thought to be a back injury that was not serious. Gronkowski ran a pair of deep pass patterns before exiting the game, and New England rallied for a 22-17 road victory as Brady found Malcolm Mitchell on an 8-yard scoring pass with 3:08 left.

A few days later, though, Gronkowski's regular season came to a sudden and abrupt end when it was announced that he would undergo back surgery to deal with a ruptured disc in his back. It would be the third time Gronkowski would undergo back surgery and increase the number of regular-season games missed over his seven-year career to 26.

There was speculation Gronkowski would be able to return in time for the postseason, but the Patriots ended any chance of that happening by putting the tight end on injured reserve. While teams are allowed to designate one player who can come off IR for the playoffs, the Patriots used that allocation on Brissett, who had undergone thumb surgery for a hit he took in Week 3 against Houston.

To the credit of Brady, Bennett and the Patriots, they did not miss a beat offensively without Gronkowski. New England won its final five games by a combined 148-53 margin, with Bennett totaling 13 receptions for 161 yards and three touchdowns.

Brady continued to operate at his unfailingly excellent levels, throwing for 1,353 yards and ten touchdowns with only one interception in those five wins. New England finished 14-2, captured its eighth consecutive AFC East title, and entered the playoffs as the number 1 seed with a bye into the divisional round.

After the Patriots had made quick work of both the Texans and Steelers to reach an NFL-record ninth Super Bowl, Gronkowski was a spectator to the greatest comeback in Super Bowl history as New England rallied from a 28-3 deficit in the final 23:31 of the second half to force overtime. The Patriots then won the coin toss to start overtime and marched 75 yards in eight plays, capped by James White's two-yard bull run for an improbable 34-28 victory that gave Brady his record fifth Super Bowl title, and arguably the sweetest of his career given how the season started with his "DeflateGate" suspension.

The second Super Bowl title of Gronkowski's career was markedly different from his first in the sense that he was a limited contributor. That differs significantly from being a minor contributor because when Gronkowski was healthy, he played at a Pro Bowl caliber. His 2016 totals of 25 catches, 540 yards, and three touchdowns were all career lows, but they were all due to unavailability as opposed to ineffectiveness.

Gronkowski will be 28 at the start of the 2017 season, which usually marks the prime years of any NFL career at a skill position besides running back. But given his multiple surgeries, there is a reason to pause. It is a fair question to ask if he can come back fully,

100 percent healthy from this procedure. While he did not play football, hockey star Mario Lemieux was plagued by chronic back pain in the later stages of his career. Lemieux's threshold of pain, though, is rightfully unquestioned given that he came back two months after being treated for Hodgkin's Disease at age 27.

Football, however, is a different animal given the constant violent nature of contact in the sport. Where in hockey, hard contact is occasional, it occurs on every play in football. And in the violent world of the NFL, every hit could also potentially be the last play of a career.

"Could he play again? Yes, definitely," Dr. Thomas Gill told NFL Network's Ian Rapoport last December. "But he'll need to take a long hard look at it, talk to his family, his surgeon, his agent, discuss whether he wants to keep playing. That's a personal decision he'll need to reflect on. He'll need to work it out with his family."

The key factor, according to Gill, is the unprecedented nature of playing after a third back surgery, at least for the Patriots. The former Patriots team doctor and Director of the Boston Sports Medicine and Research Institute did not rule out Gronkowski being able to return, but he also noted that "in sports medicine, past performance is a predictor of the future."

Gronkowski still has three years and $24 million remaining on the six-year contract extension he signed before the 2013 season, with the latter figure a very salary cap-friendly number. By putting him on injured reserve, the Patriots took away any chance of Gronkowski rushing through his rehab to return to play, something that ruined J.J. Watt's season for the Texans. In hindsight, this was probably the best decision for both the team and Gronkowski.

And in 2017, the Patriots are likely going to need Gronkowski since he is expected to be the primary pass-catching tight end. Bennett parlayed his Super Bowl title into a three-year, $21 million contract with the Green Bay Packers that included a $6.3 million signing bonus. The Patriots did sign Dwayne Allen from the Colts in the offseason in hopes he could fill Bennett's spot. For his part, Gronkowski has been diligent about his rehab process according to ESPN's Mike Reiss in late March.

"A few (players) have stayed in the area and are working out regularly at the team's facility. Most notable on the list is tight end Rob Gronkowski, whose recovery from back surgery continues to progress. Gronkowski has been at the stadium at least four days a week, joining a few other teammates who are also rehabbing, such as running back Dion Lewis. ... While Gronkowski often generates headlines for his off-field endeavors – such as a recent trip to Barcelona – often overlooked is his work ethic and commitment in the weight room and conditioning-wise. Few work harder than him."

Chapter 6: Rob Gronkowski's Personal Life

Robert James Gronkowski has always been a fun-loving individual. Ever since his college days in Arizona, he has had a reputation as a partygoer. Whether it be dancing up a storm or simply hitting the party scene, Gronkowski is a fixture in Internet memes, articles, and videos.

He revealed in a July 2015 interview on "CBS This Morning" that partying is his way of unwinding. Football is a tough sport. It requires year-round preparation both on and off the field. Whenever they are not on the gridiron, players are expected to study and master their playbook. Gronkowski is no exception. He told CBS that a good party now and then makes him a better football player.[xcviii]

"It makes you get that itch to go back out," he said. "You go out and get refreshed, and it just makes you want to go back out on that practice field and keep going hard."

"When you get that itch," he added. "When you're working for like 20 days in a row, you're out on the practice field just grinding; you want to go out once in a while."

His teammate, Patriots quarterback and three-time Super Bowl MVP Tom Brady, wrote a statement for "CBS This Morning." In it, Brady lauded Gronkowski for his optimism and authenticity.

"Gronk is a one of a kind person, player, and friend," Brady said. "He is one of the most positive people I have ever been around, and he loves to have fun. What you see is what you get, and whether he is dancing, singing, laughing, or spiking, he is true to himself."

Gronkowski revealed in his 2015 book, *It's Good to be Gronk*, that nobody can compare to him and his brothers when it comes to partying. When Gronkowski is moving and flailing his body at parties, he considers it a workout.[xcix]

"Okay, here's the deal," Gronkowski wrote. "Football season was over, it had its ups and downs, but I had busted my butt, and now it was time to move forward. That meant it was time to train for next season and party for tonight. The good thing about the way me and my brothers party is that we don't sit on our butts or just stand around with drinks in our hands. We go hard! We don't do drugs; we don't need to."

"Because when we get started, we party harder than anybody," he continued. "We are dancing high-energy, constant moves, jumping, gyrations – it is the best cardio workout ever. So actually, even when I am partying, I am working out."

Gronkowski also hit the party scene with then-Cleveland Browns rookie quarterback Johnny Manziel in May 2014. After Browns organized team activities (OTAs) concluded that week, Manziel went to Las Vegas to watch UFC 173. The same weekend, he hung out with the New England Patriots tight end at a pool party at the DAYLIGHT Beach Club in Mandalay Bay.[c]

Gronkowski's love for partying is also evident in his two endeavors, "The Gronk Bus" and "Gronk's Party Ship."

When he was just eight years old, he told his family that he would purchase a limousine bus one day. That vision became a reality some 15 years or so later. His family now owns "The Gronk Party Bus," a Ford F550 limo bus which can fit as many as 25 passengers. According to the bus' official website, Rob Gronkowski designed it himself.[ci]

The Gronkowskis rent the bus to various partygoers. "If you are a true New England Sports fan, the Gronk Bus will be one of the greatest experiences you will find," per TheGronkBus.com. "Whether it's a wedding, Patriots game, or a prom, the Gronk Bus will hype up your event like no other."

"The Gronk Party Bus" features include a football field-lighted ceiling, Rob Gronkowski's portrait on lighted acrylic, New England Patriots themed colors (blue, red, and white), 43-inch flat screen television, premium sound system, and restroom.

According to AZCentral.com's Bob McManaman, Gronkowski and his family regularly bring "The Gronk Party Bus" whenever they tailgate before a Patriots game. The family also hired a personal chef, Joe Papa. He whipped up delicious food for the 2014 AFC Divisional Round game against the Baltimore Ravens.[cii]

"The menu at a recent playoff game against the Ravens included 20 pounds of beef tips, 10 pounds of chicken, and $300 worth of Chinese food," says McManaman.

Apparently, a bus is not enough for Rob Gronkowski's party habits.

The Gronkowski family's "Gronk's Party Ship" set sail on its inaugural cruise from Miami, FL to Nassau, Bahamas from February 19-22, 2016. According to the ship's official website (GronksPartyShip.com), among the celebrities in attendance were Flo Rida, Redfoo, 3Lau, Waka Flocka Flame, Sammy Adams, Brooke Evers, Brazzabelle, Dante, Costa, Finesse Mitchell, Robert Powell, Matt Rife, and The Big Rock Show.[ciii]

"Gronk's Party Ship" is a Norwegian Pearl model. It has ten types of staterooms, ten restaurants, a bowling alley, spa, fitness center, sports court, Internet café, hot tubs, jogging track, and several boutiques.

As hard of a party animal Rob Gronkowski is, he also does other interesting things in the public eye.

He made his movie debut in a cameo role for "Entourage" in March 2014. He appeared with Patriots teammate and wide receiver Julian Edelman. The two New England Patriots players were in a one-second beach party scene appearance.[civ]

In June 2015, the New England tight end told SI.com's Jake Fischer he had a lot of fun filming "Entourage." He singled out "Vinny" as the movie character he could relate to the most.[cv]

"'Entourage' was great," Gronkowski said. "I filmed that over a year ago, and it went super smooth, super well. Every part I shot made the movie which is very, very cool and it was just a great experience, and I loved watching the shows growing up. I was just super excited to hear about the movie and just being in it. So it was definitely an honor, no doubt."

"I would have to go with Vince, Vinny," he continued. "The way he rolls with the crew and everything. I feel like I could fit in with any of them just the way they roll and the way they are. But if I had to be one of the characters, I would definitely be Vinny."

Gronkowski and his family also appeared on "Family Feud," a long-running daytime game show, in July 2015. Gronkowski took the lead for his side. They went up against former NFL quarterback Rodney Peete and his family.[cvi] At the time, the Patriots were embroiled in the infamous "DeflateGate" scandal where quarterback Tom Brady allegedly conspired with two locker room attendants to deflate the game balls that were used for the 2014 AFC Championship Game against the Indianapolis Colts. Two months before the Gronkowskis appeared on "Family Feud," NFL commissioner Roger Goodell issued a four-game suspension on Brady. The league also slapped the Patriots with a $1 million fine and forfeited two draft picks from them. Goodell upheld this suspension a week after the Gronkowskis' game-show stint, only to have a U.S. District Judge overturn it in September.

When it was Rob Gronkowski's turn to face off against Holly Robinson-Peete on "Family Feud," host Steve Harvey asked, "Name something that can be inflated or deflated." *New York Daily News'* writer Amara Grautski described it as a "blatant reference to DeflateGate."

Ms. Peete answered first. She said, "A balloon." When Harvey looked at Gronkowski for his response, the Patriots tight end said, "I don't even want this one."

"I'm going to have to answer questions all the time," he continued.

Harvey then replied, "Stay away from this one, kid."

The Peete family emerged victorious in the end. Despite the loss, Rob Gronkowski was still being Rob Gronkowski. He showed his famous dance moves to the "Family Feud" studio audience, and they gave him thunderous applause.

Less than a year later, Gronkowski showed that he has a soft spot for children.

According to Angelique Fiske of the Patriots' official website, Gronkowski agreed to be the host of a Nickelodeon children's television show entitled "Crashletes" in March 2016.[cvii]

"It's about athletes that didn't make it pro," Gronkowski told ThePostGame.com (via Patriots.com). "We're showing them fall, wipe out, making jokes about it. We're just having a blast. We're having a fun time."

Aside from Gronkowski's various television appearances, he also endorses several products. Many companies became attracted to his appeal after his breakout sophomore year in the pro ranks.

Gronkowski signed his first product endorsement in February 2012. He signed a deal with renowned bodybuilding supplement company, Six Star Pro Nutrition. Gronkowski raved about the benefits of the company's protein supplements for athletes. In a press release that MuscleAndFitness.com obtained, Gronkowski's deal covers media in print, digital, and social forms.[cviii]

Oklahoma City Thunder point guard Russell Westbrook and Miami Marlins outfielder Mike Stanton (now known as Giancarlo Stanton) were the other athletes who signed the Six Star Pro Nutrition endorsement deal along with Gronkowski.

Gronkowski then signed a two-year deal with Dunkin' Donuts in March 2012. The contract stipulates that he will endorse the company's products and appear in its television, radio, and social media advertisements. Other past New England Patriots players who served as Dunkin' Donuts endorsers include Tom Brady, Wes Welker, Tedy Bruschi, and Adam Vinatieri.[cix]

Five months after inking the Dunkin' Donuts deal, Gronkowski became an investor and partner of BodyArmor Sports Drink. According to *Forbes Magazine's* Lance Madden, Gronkowski's role "could include product testing, charitable support, regional and community events, and national advertising."[cx]

In a press release Madden obtained, Gronkowski reiterated his commitment to fitness and health. The Patriots' star tight end said that he loves the benefits and taste of BodyArmor Sports Drink.

In September 2012, Gronkowski's famous "Gronk Flakes," a breakfast cereal, hit Stop & Shop shelves in the New England area. PLB Sports is the manufacturer of the product. Its president and CEO, Ty Ballou, told ESPN that Gordy Gronkowski, Sr. approached the company in 2010 asking that his three NFL-playing sons – Dan, Chris, and Rob – be featured in one of its products. In the end, only Rob Gronkowski emerged as company product endorser after his huge second year in the NFL. Proceeds of his "Gronk Flakes" go to the Gronk National Youth Foundation.[cxi]

PLB Sports also created Detroit Tigers pitcher Justin Verlander's "Fastball Flakes."

Gronkowski also endorsed fantasy sports companies DraftKings and FanDuel in December 2014.[cxii]

A month later, Gronkowski became a Brand Ambassador of SMS Audio, a company which produces audio headphones and accessories. Gronkowski said that his ideal fitness gear also includes headphones, which help him maximize every workout. He singled out SMS Audio's BioSport heart-rate monitoring earbuds as his favorite.[cxiii]

Nine months after the New England Patriots won Super Bowl XLIX, Gronkowski signed an endorsement contract with Monster Energy Drink – the second-biggest in the U.S. market. In a statement, the New England tight end labeled it as "the ultimate deal for me." He also said the product is a good fit for his personality. Gronkowski ended his more than three-year partnership with BodyArmor in the process. ESPN's Darren Rovell reported in November 2015 that Gronkowski still maintained his shares with BodyArmor despite the termination of his endorsement deal with the company.[cxiv]

Rob Gronkowski made a sound life decision when he turned down a $4 million disability insurance policy when he injured his back in his sophomore year at the University of Arizona. His frugality has carried into his life as a professional NFL player.

According to his 2015 autobiography, *It's Good to be Gronk*, he has not spent any of his earnings from his NFL career. When the book came out in the summer, he had been playing professionally for five years. At that point, his lifetime earnings were $10 million. Instead, Gronkowski is making a living off his endorsement deals.

He reveals he is not into expensive cars or jewelry. He even backs up what his father Gordy, Sr. said after he signed his six-year, $54 million in 2013. Rob Gronkowski is still the same guy he was when he was in high school in Western New York and Western Pennsylvania. As a matter of fact, Gronkowski said he still wears his favorite pair of high-school jeans.[cxv]

Aside from Gronkowski's endorsements, he is also active in several business ventures.

He is involved in the family fitness business, "Gronkowski Fitness Equipment." Its main website attributes its beginnings to the family's fitness background and Gordy Gronkowski, Sr.'s 25 years of experience in the industry. Among the fitness equipment they sell and manufacture are power racks, benches, weights, pull-up bars, plyo boxes, rowers, attachment bars, battle ropes, power sleds, and fitness balls. The company also sells recovery products such as foam rollers, body sticks, and massage balls.[cxvi]

"Gronkowski Fitness Equipment" is advertised on the GronkNation.com website. Gordy Gronkowski's fitness business, G&G Fitness, is also featured. The other family endeavors – "The Gronk Bus" as well as Chris Gronkowski and his girlfriend's online engraving business ("Everything Decorated") – are advertised as well.

Rob Gronkowski and his family also make it a point to give back to their community. He and his brothers founded the Gronk Nation Youth Foundation. According to its official website, the Gronkowskis have "been giving back to the community since they started playing sports." The foundation's mission is to assist young people to be active in school and sports. It also aims to provide these youngsters with tools to help them achieve their dreams.[cxvii]

Every June, Rob Gronkowski shaves his head as a show of support for "One Mission Buzz Off for Kids with Cancer" at Gillette Stadium. Every August, his Foundation takes part in the New Balance Falmouth Road Race in Cape Cod. Proceeds from the race go to programs in need of safe sports equipment. The event will celebrate its 43rd running in August 2016. Other charitable institutions which the Gronk Nation Youth Foundation supports include The Boston Marathon, The Charity Xbox Challenge, and The Citi Rob Gronkowski Football Clinic.

Gronkowski hosts his annual two-day football clinic in June for children in the first to eighth grades. Each camper receives a Rob Gronkowski autograph, t-shirt, and team photo. Part of the camp's proceeds go to the Gronk Nation Youth Foundation, per the former's official website.[cxviii]

Gronkowski also hosted his third annual women's football clinic in September 2015.[cxix]

As for Rob Gronkowski's love life, it has gone mainly under the radar.

In a February 2015 tweet (via CBS Sports), Gronkowski said, "Sometimes chicks are crazy...I don't got a girlfriend." His followers re-tweeted the statement more than 10 thousand times.

At the time, he finished hosting an event in Connecticut with model Marisa Hunter. The latter posted a photo of herself and Gronkowski at the said event on her Twitter account. Many speculated that the two were dating or had dated. However, they were not together, per CBS Sports' John Breech.[cxx]

An October 2015 update reveals that Gronkowski was dating former New England Patriots cheerleader Camille Kostek. The latter had been a long-time Patriots fan as she hails from

Killingworth, CT (just a two-hour drive from Gillette Stadium in Foxborough, Mass.). According to Heavy.com's Tim Keeney, Kostek was a Patriots cheerleader from 2013-15. She started dating Gronkowski in April 2015, and they went public with their relationship five months later.[cxxi]

The 23-year-old Kostek confirmed she and Gronkowski had been dating to *The Boston Globe*.[cxxii]

However, it proved to be a short-lived relationship.

PageSix.com's Carlos Greer reported in January 2016 that Kostek had been in an on-and-off relationship with American Idol Season 14 winner and fellow Connecticut native Nick Fradiani. A source told Greer that Fradiani met Kostek when he was on his American Idol promotional tour. The same source also said he spotted the two spending New Year's Eve 2015 together.[cxxiii]

In a February 2016 interview with E! News, Gronkowski confirmed that he is unattached. He said he did not have any plans for Valentine's Day in the days leading up to his "Gronk's Party Ship" cruise to the Bahamas and Nassau. Back then, Gronkowski was trying to stay in shape by doing strength training, boxing, and playing basketball.

He also confirmed that he had plans of appearing on ABC's "Dancing with the Stars." The studio had yet to reach out to him, but he said it was no big deal considering his busy schedule revolving around his fitness and football regimen.[cxxiv]

For a busy 26-year-old bachelor such as NFL Pro Bowl and Super Bowl-winning tight end Robert James Gronkowski, life does not get any better.

Chapter 7 -- Gronkowski's Legacy

It is always difficult to speculate on a player's legacy, more so in the case of Rob Gronkowski because not only is he still playing in the NFL, but he is also entering what would be considered the prime of his career at age 28 come May. The vast litany of injuries he has already endured have cost him the equivalent of 1 ½ seasons over his seven-year career, which puts his production to date all the more astounding.

Despite playing in only 88 regular-season games since being drafted in 2010, Gronkowski ranks fifth among all tight ends with 405 catches in that span. His 6,095 receiving yards trail only Jimmy Graham (6,280), and his 68 scoring receptions and 15.0 yards per catch top all players at the position.

Two of the four players above Gronkowski in receptions are sure-fire Hall of Famers – Tony Witten of the Dallas Cowboys and Antonio Gates of the San Diego and soon to be Los Angeles Chargers. Both have enjoyed stellar standout careers with Witten ranking second in all tight ends to Tony Gonzalez with 1,089 catches for 11,888 yards. Gates, who has 111 TD catches, will pass Gonzalez for the most by a tight end with his first one of 2017. He also has a chance to overtake Witten for receiving yards, entering this season 696 behind the Cowboys star.

But their styles are as different as night and day. Witten is a throwback tight end, the guy who lines up on the end of the line and does most of his damage over the middle between the hash marks and occasionally breaking tackles to rip off big gains. Despite his incredible 14-year career to date, Witten has five fewer receiving touchdowns (63) than Gronkowski.

Gates, however, took after Gonzalez in the fact that he played basketball in college before transitioning to the NFL. While Gonzalez was a two-sport star at Cal and well-versed at tight end when he was the 13th overall selection in the 1997 NFL Draft by the Kansas City Chiefs, the 6-foot-5 Gates had no such grounding in college football.

He was an undersized power forward at Kent State and averaged 16.0 points and 8.1 rebounds as a junior in helping the Golden Flashes reach the Elite Eight of the 2002 NCAA Tournament as a number 10 seed, eventually losing to Indiana. He averaged 20.6 points and 7.7 rebounds the following season, but Kent State only reached the NIT in the postseason.

Since 6-foot-5 power forwards are not in high demand in the NBA unless your name is Charles Barkley, Gates turned his attention back to football. Originally he had hoped to play at Michigan State, but scheduling conflicts prevented him from playing both sports, which resulted in his eventual landing spot at Kent State.

His basketball skills translated well to football, and his athleticism created all sorts of problems for opponents. Like Gronkowski, Gates has an enormous catch radius, the ability to run precise routes and also the ability to box out defenders when making a catch on the run. He became the best Chargers tight end since another Hall of Famer named Kellen Winslow, one of the pioneers of the position when it came to freakish athleticism.

Comparing Gronkowski to Gates or Gonzalez is more of an apples to apples comparison than to Witten, who is a throwback tight end in the sense he is rarely, if ever, deployed anywhere but at the end of the line between the hash marks. Gronkowski, Gates, and Gonzalez, as well as Seattle Seahawks tight end Jimmy Graham, have been used at the usual tight end spot as well as slot receivers or in the standard wide receiver position.

The Patriots also have adjusted their offense on a year-to-year basis, part of the pragmatic approach Belichick has for winning games on a week-to-week basis. In Gronkowski's rookie season, the Patriots ranked 25th in the NFL by passing the ball 54.7 percent of the time. As Gronkowski became a bigger part of the offense the following season, that number jumped to 58.9 percent, which ranked 11th.

The next four years, the Patriots threw the ball at least 57 percent of the time in each season, but from 2012-14, they ranked no higher than 16th. This was in part because of the league's offensive evolution away from the running game. In 2015, however, the Patriots threw the ball on 65 percent of their plays, partly out of necessity since they did not have a consistent running game. To wit, LeGarrette Blount did not crack 1,000 yards in a season with the Patriots until this past campaign.

And through it all, the Patriots have maintained their stranglehold on the AFC East, partly due to the ineffectiveness of Buffalo, Miami, and the New York Jets, but also because they have just been a dominant team with a future Hall of Famer at quarterback and head coach. In Gronkowski's seven years as a pro, the Patriots have won no fewer than 12 games in a season and have reached the AFC title game each of the last six years. Gronkowski has been an integral part of that machine, and if he stays healthy, he has the chance to add more Super Bowl titles to his resume in addition to bolstering his statistics.

Brady will serve as the tide that lifts all boats in the Hall of Fame argument when it comes to Patriots players who will be enshrined in Canton. But when you list all of the premier tight ends in the past 40 years, starting with Ozzie Newsome, and then Winslow and Gonzalez, Witten, Gates and Graham, who can be argued is the closest thing to Gronkowski's peer since they were in the same draft class and have roughly the same physique (Graham is 6-foot-7 and weighs 265 pounds), the only person in this group who has a Super Bowl ring is Gronkowski. And he has two.

In fact, following Graham and Gronkowski over the rest of their careers could serve as the litmus test for the other regarding who gets to the Hall of Fame first should they retire together – which of course, is not guaranteed to happen. But Graham has thus far been far more durable than Gronkowski, having played all but seven of a possible 112 games in his seven-year career.

In fact, Graham is one reception shy of becoming the 13th tight end in NFL history with 500 receptions. But he has amassed only 185 more yards than Gronkowski in those 17 extra games and has nine fewer TD catches (59).

To have a 6-foot-6, 265-pound target be able to catch passes over the middle is a requirement in today's NFL. Gronkowski, however, can create separation from a linebacker while running his route. This is one area where he stands apart from peers at his position.

Gronkowski can also run a seam route starting in the slot and outrun his coverage for mid-range and deep passes. There are only a select few in the league who can do that now, and only Graham does it on a level with Gronkowski.

In a 2015 story in Sports Illustrated about Gronkowski, Garoppolo revealed an interesting insight. Gronkowski has a wide receiver's ability to "burst in and out of routes. Most big guys, it takes them a while to start and stop. He is really an offensive tackle with wide receiver speed."

Brady added his take on this point in an interview with Business Insider later that year, noting, "He's got great speed. I don't know what he was timed when he came out of college, but he gives great body language when he runs. I can really tell when he really starts to accelerate, and he feels like he can run by the guy that is on him."

That speed becomes apparent when he is isolated against either a linebacker or safety in single coverage. The phrase "if he's even, he's leaving," applies to Gronkowski when he runs deep seam routes because he can separate from coverage and make catches over the middle for big gains.

Additionally, he is a fearless receiver. There has never been a play where Gronkowski could be accused of "alligator-arming" or hearing footsteps when going over the middle on a pass. That's partly because Brady would probably excoriate him, or anyone else, in the huddle after the play, but Gronkowski has never shied from contact. Rather, it is the opposite in his case – he has loved it throughout his career -- and to praise Seahawks safety Earl Thomas after a hit that nearly collapsed a lung and eventually forced him to miss New England's last five regular-season games and the Super Bowl run only reinforces that belief.

The versatility Gronkowski brings to his pass-catching is unprecedented. It is one thing to have a large catch radius, something Gronkowski has because of his 6-foot-6 height, but to have someone that large be a viable sideline target on a back-shoulder throw borders on unfair to defenses. And that throw has replaced the down-and-out pattern for quarterbacks since the ball arrives quicker and gives the cornerback or safety less time to turn and potentially make a play on the ball.

Lastly, Gronkowski's work ethic is not to be underappreciated. When a player is unique and creates mismatches the way he does, a good team figures out ways to exploit those mismatches for its benefit. And a good player puts the work in at practice, in the weight room, and in the film room to make sure he can continue to create those mismatches to exploit. And throughout his football career at every stop, Gronkowski has been a willing worker. He has also had to be a willing worker to recover fully from each injury he has suffered in his career.

That work ethic is why he is able to enjoy playing football, injuries notwithstanding. He probably caused Patriots fans a few nervy moments at WrestleMania 33 when he got into the ring and dropped wrestler Jinder Mahal with a hit coming out of a three-point stance. But the desire to be the consummate teammate rings true to Gronkowski, and that means he gets plenty of motivation putting the work in to be part of the Super Bowl title defense in 2017.

"Just being there supporting the guys, it was unbelievable," he told NFL.com at WrestleMania. "They worked super hard. And it was awesome just to be a part of it. But (it) definitely motivates me to get back out on the field. Just seeing how hard they worked, all the efforts they put in, being part of it just makes me want to keep grinding, keep on going and I've definitely hit the rehab hard. And I'm going to make sure when I hit the field this year I'm super ready to go. So definitely (it) motivated me big time to get back out there, so we can get out there with the boys and do it again."

Conclusion

It turns out that Gordy Gronkowski, Sr.'s venture into the fitness equipment business did his fourth son, Rob, a lot of good.

As Rob Gronkowski mentioned, getting immersed in a competitive environment at home which revolved around fitness helped prepare him for the many battles he faced later in life. His grit and determination stemmed from those early years in Amherst, NY when he competed with his four brothers to see who could lift the heaviest and produce the best stats in whatever sports they played. Beneath his easy-going persona lies a person who has gone through so much. He was the victim of a high-school e-mail prank, an ineligible high-school football player transfer, the son of divorced parents, and a player who has gone through a countless assortment of injuries in college and the NFL. Living a fit lifestyle has taught Rob Gronkowski to take out his frustrations in the weight room and remain confident no matter what he goes through in life. It is a lesson he carries on to the present moment, and one can be sure he will do so for the rest of his life.

Gronkowski's patience on the field has paid dividends. He has all the physical tools for a tight end – size, catching ability, blocking ability, and agility. However, if he did not put all of the work in, none of these would have mattered. Many NFL superstars took their opportunities for granted. They thought they could get by with talent alone, but they were wrong. To succeed in the NFL, you have to combine talent with commitment, hard work, relentlessness, and dedication. Rob Gronkowski was able to do that. Hard evidence of this is his numerous accolades from the high school to the professional level. All of these trophies are neatly displayed in his father Gordy, Sr.'s cabinet in his Amherst, NY basement.

Don't forget the numerous NFL records he broke for tight ends, either. Without a doubt, the pinnacle was Gronkowski's first Super Bowl ring. With Gronkowski, Tom Brady, and head coach Bill Belichick around, it is a safe bet they are primed to win more.

Gronkowski has also admitted that partying is an integral part of his life. People can judge him to be just some millionaire party animal, but this is just part of the whole scheme of things. Partying is one of his outlets. It is his way of blowing off steam after going through a rigorous grind known as the National Football League. Would he have been the deadly, four-time Pro

Bowl tight end he is, had he not been the person he is? Probably not. Many are afraid to be themselves for fear of others judging them, but not Rob Gronkowski. He has never been afraid to be himself, whether it be in real life or on social media. His family, the New England Patriots, the fans, the parties, the workouts, the "Gronk Spikes," the endorsements, the television and movie appearances, and the charitable endeavors – these make up the real Rob Gronkowski. In spite of his continued success, he has remained true to himself. He has also remained humble. Hard evidence of this is him living off his endorsements instead of his NFL salary. We live in an age where many athletes flaunt their riches and accomplishments. Rob Gronkowski could have chosen to do this, but he did not.

Gronkowski has an autobiography. His father, Gordy, Sr., has also written a book (*Growing Up Gronk*). Consider the fact that Gronkowski will be just 27 years old in May 2016. He could end up playing in the NFL for another decade, and maybe more. Having said that, there is still more to learn about Rob Gronkowski as the years go by. It is a safe bet that he could write another autobiography once he finishes his NFL career, wins more Super Bowl trophies, sells more fitness equipment, goes to more parties, raises more money for charity, and eventually raises a family of his own (if he so chooses to). That is something that any NFL fan – not just New England Patriots fans – should anticipate.

Whatever the case may be, he will still just be Rob Gronkowski – a fun-loving guy who has lived life his way. As we have discovered, it has been a life well lived so far.

Final Word/About the Author

I was born and raised in Norwalk, Connecticut. Growing up, I could often be found spending many nights watching basketball, soccer, and football matches with my father in the family living room. I love sports and everything that sports can embody. I believe that sports are one of most genuine forms of competition, heart, and determination. I write my works to learn more about influential athletes in the hopes that from my writing, you the reader can walk away inspired to put in an equal if not greater amount of hard work and perseverance to pursue your goals. If you enjoyed *Rob Gronkowski: The Inspiring Story of One of Football's Greatest Tight Ends*, please leave a review! Also, you can read more of my works on *Roger Federer, Novak Djokovic, Andrew Luck, Brett Favre, Calvin Johnson, Drew Brees, J.J. Watt, Colin Kaepernick, Aaron Rodgers, Peyton Manning, Tom Brady, Russell Wilson, Michael Jordan, LeBron James, Kyrie Irving, Klay Thompson, Stephen Curry, Kevin Durant, Russell Westbrook, Anthony Davis, Chris Paul, Blake Griffin, Kobe Bryant, Joakim Noah, Scottie Pippen, Carmelo Anthony, Kevin Love, Grant Hill, Tracy McGrady, Vince Carter, Patrick Ewing, Karl Malone, Tony Parker, Allen Iverson, Hakeem Olajuwon, Reggie Miller, Michael Carter-Williams, John Wall, James Harden, Tim Duncan, Steve Nash,*

Draymond Green, Kawhi Leonard, Dwyane Wade, Ray Allen, Pau Gasol, Dirk Nowitzki, Jimmy Butler, Paul Pierce, Manu Ginobili, Pete Maravich, Larry Bird, Kyle Lowry, Jason Kidd, David Robinson, LaMarcus Aldridge, Derrick Rose, Paul George, Kevin Garnett, Chris Paul, Marc Gasol, Yao Ming, Al Horford and Amar'e Stoudemire in the Kindle Store. If you love basketball, check out my website at claytongeoffreys.com to join my exclusive list where I let you know about my latest books and give you lots of goodies.

Like what you read? Please leave a review!

I write because I love sharing the stories of influential people like Rob Gronkowski with fantastic readers like you. My readers inspire me to write more so please do not hesitate to let me know what you thought by leaving a review! If you love books on life, sports, or productivity, check out my website at claytongeoffreys.com to join my exclusive list where I let you know about my latest books. Aside from being the first to hear about my latest releases, you can also download a free copy of *33 Life Lessons: Success Principles, Career Advice & Habits of Successful People*. See you there!

Clayton

References

[i] "Rob, New England Patriots." Gronknation.com/Rob. Web.

[ii] Tarapacki, Thomas. "How the Gronkowskis Grew Up." *The Am-Pol Eagle*. 24 September 2013. Web.

[iii] Wuebben, Joe. "Gronk'd: Getting Personal with the Gronkowskis." *Men's Fitness Magazine*. Web.

[iv] "Gordon Gronkowski." Baseball-Reference.com. Web.

[v] "Dan Gronkowski." NFL.com 2009 draft. Web.

[vi] Kent, Andy. "Rob Gronkowski's Brothers Seeking Another NFL Chance." NFL.com. 24 March 2014. Web.

[vii] Dunne, Tyler. "One More Gronk to Go: Glenn Gronkowski Poised to Make Impact in NFL." *The Buffalo News*. 31 January 2016. Web.

[viii] "Glenn Gronkowski." "2016 NFL Draft Prospects." NFL.com. Web.

[ix] Weber, Bruce. "How Rob Gronkowski's Dad Raised America's First Family of Jocks." *Vanity Fair Magazine*. 9 December 2015. Web.

[x] Daniels, Mark. "Gronkowski Reflects on Football as He Heads Home to Buffalo." *Providence Journal*. 11 October 2014. Web.

[xii] Jones, Chris. "One Thousand Two Hundred and Fifty-Eight Pounds of Sons." *Esquire Magazine*. 6 June 2014. Web.

[xiii] MacMullan, Jackie. "It's Good to be Gronk." ESPN Boston. 12 January 2012. Web.

[xiv] "Rob Gronkowski Bio." ArizonaWildcats.com. Web.

[xv] Dunlap, Colin. "PIAA Reverses WPIAL, Rules Player Eligible." *The Pittsburgh Post-Gazette*. 25 August 2006. Web.

[xvi] White, Mike. "WPIAL Benches High School Football Transfer." *The Pittsburgh Post-Gazette*. 22 August 2006. Web.

[xvii] Dononue, Tyler. "The College Recruitment of Rob Gronkowski." Bleacher Report. 29 September 2015. Web.

[xviii] "Arizona vs. Oregon – Box Score – November 15, 2008 – ESPN." ESPN. Web.

[xix] Arizona Athletics. "Gronkowski on Early National Radar." ArizonaWildcats.com. 2 March 2009. Web.

xx "Strained Back Sidelines Gronkowski." *The Associated Press* (via ESPN.com). 19 September 2009. Web.

xxi Gronkowski, Rob. "Gronk's Biggest Gamble." MMQB.SI.com. 15 July 2015. Web.

xxii "2010 NFL Combine Results." NFLcombineresults.com. Web.

xxiii "Rob Gronkowski TE Arizona." NFL.com Scouting Combine Profiles. Web.

xxiv Breer, Albert. "Gronkowski Combine Numbers." Boston.com. 24 April 2010. Web.

xxv Reiss, Mike. "Combine Played Role in Patriots Gaining Comfort with Rob Gronkowski." ESPN Boston. 23 February 2016. Web.

xxvi Hensley, Jamison. "Ravens Taking a Close Look at Injured Prospects." *The Baltimore Sun.* 17 April 2010. Web.

xxvii Kolko, Dan. "Revisiting the Gronkowski-Kindle Draft Day Sequence." MASNSports.com. 17 January 2012. Web.

xxviii Hill, Rich. "9 Days to the Draft: Arizona TE, Rob Gronkowski." PatsPulpit.com. 13 April 2010. Web.

xxix Volin, Ben. "Rob Gronkowski's First Back Rehab Detailed in Book." *The Boston Globe.* 4 August 2013. Web.

xxx Nagy, Patrick J. "Gronkowski Brothers Join NFL Ranks." *Amherst Bee.* 28 April 2010. Web.

xxxi "Rob Gronkowski – New England Patriots." Pyromaniac.com. Web.

xxxii "New England Patriots History." JT-SW.com. Web.

xxxiii "Tom Brady Throws 2 TDs to Wes Welker as Patriots Cruise." 12 September 2010. Web.

xxxiv "Player Game Finder Query Results." Pro-FootballReference.com. Web.

xxxv "Tom Brady Makes History as Patriots Lock Up AFC's No. 1 Seed." ESPN. 27 December 2010. Web.

xxxvi "Rob Gronkowski Game-by-Game Stats." ESPN. Web.

xxxvii "Mark Sanchez Tosses 3 TDs as Jets Soar into AFC Title Game." ESPN. 17 January 2011. Web.

xxxviii "Tom Brady Picks Apart Dolphins as 517-Yard, 4 TD Opener Fuels Pats." ESPN. 13 September 2011. Web.

xxxix "Pats Bury Chiefs After Shaky 1st as Tom Brady, Rob Gronkowski Shine Again." ESPN. 22 November 2011. Web.

[xl] "Gronkowski Scores 3 Touchdowns to Lead Patriots Past Colts." ESPN. 4 December 2011. Web.

[xli] "Patriots Clinch No. 1 Seed in AFC With Win Over Bills." ESPN. 1 January 2012. Web.

[xlii] Kuharsky, Paul. "All-Pro Voting Totals." ESPN. 6 January 2012. Web.

[xliii] "Tom Brady Fuels Record Night as Pats End Tim Tebow's Run with Rout." ESPN. 15 January 2012. Web.

[xliv] "Tom Brady, Missed FG Vault Patriots Past Stunned Ravens, into Super Bowl." ESPN. 23 January 2012. Web.

[xlv] Florio, Mike. "Gronkowski Will Play." Pro Football Talk. 4 February 2012. Web.

[xlvi] Somers, Kent. "Super Bowl XLVI: Rob Gronkowski a 'Competitive Fool.'" *The Arizona Republic*. 3 February 2012. Web.

[xlvii] Reiss, Mike. "Can Patriots Deal with 'Gronk Effect?' ESPN. 1 February 2012. Web.

[xlviii] Rodak, Mike. "Hobbled Gronk not his Super Self." ESPN. 6 February 2012. Web.

[xlix] Pepin, Matt. "Rob Gronkowski Has Ankle Surgery." *The Boston Globe*. 10 February 2012.

[l] "New Video Shows Gronkowski, Light Dancing at Post-Super Bowl Party." CBS Boston. 7 February 2012. Web.

[li] Tasch, Justin. "Rob Gronkowski Doesn't Want to Revisit Patriots' Loss to Giants in Super Bowl XLVI." *The New York Daily News*. 12 November 2015. Web.

[lii] "Rob Gronkowski Gets 6-Year Deal." ESPN. 8 June 2012. Web.

[liii] Breer, Albert and Rapoport, Ian. "Patriots, Rob Gronkowski Agree to Six-Year, $54M Extension." NFL.com. 8 June 2012. Web.

[liv] "Tom Brady, Pats Score Six Straight TDs in 2nd Half, KO Bills." ESPN. 30 September 2012. Web.

[lv] "Tom Brady Outshines Andrew Luck as Pats Score 59 on Colts." ESPN. 19 November 2012. Web.

[lvi] "Rob Gronkowski has Surgery." ESPN. 19 November 2012. Web.

[lvii] "Aaron Hernandez Game-by-Game Stats." ESPN. Web.

[lviii] "Rob Gronkowski Returns as Patriots Blank Dolphins to Earn Playoff Bye." ESPN. 31 December 2012. Web.

[lix] Rosenthal, Gregg. "Rob Gronkowski Breaks Left Forearm, out for

Playoffs." NFL.com. 14 January 2013. Web.

lx "Tom Brady Wins QB-Record 17th Playoff Game as Pats Advance." ESPN. 14 January 2013. Web.

lxi "Ravens Defeat Patriots, Set Up Harbaugh Battle in Super Bowl." ESPN. 21 January 2013. Web.

lxii "Rob Gronkowski had Infection in Arm." ESPN. 26 February 2013. Web.

lxiii "Surgery Likely for Rob Gronkowski." ESPN Boston. 8 April 2013. Web.

lxiv "Source: Gronkowski's Infection Gone." ESPN Boston. 21 May 2013. Web.

lxv Garafolo, Mike. "Doctors Optimistic Rob Gronkowski (Back Surgery) will Return for Week 1." *USA Today Sports*. 19 June 2013. Web.

lxvi Pelissero, Tom. "Patriots' Gronkowski Cleared to Play vs. Jets." *USA Today Sports*. 18 October 2013. Web.

lxvii "Jets Stun Patriots on Nick Folk FG after Controversial Call in OT." ESPN. 20 October 2013. Web.

lxviii "Tom Brady Tosses 4 TD Passes as Patriots Trounce Steelers." ESPN. 5 November 2013. Web.

lxix "Patriots Beat Browns with Two Touchdowns in Final 61 Seconds." ESPN. 9 December 2013. Web.

lxx "Rob Gronkowski Out; Tears ACL, MCL." ESPN. 10 December 2013. Web.

lxxi Sessler, Marc. "Rob Gronkowski Out for Season with Torn ACL, MCL." NFL.com. 10 December 2013. Web.

lxxii "Patriots Release Tight End Aaron Hernandez." Patriots.com. 26 June 2013. Web.

lxxiii Reiss, Mike. "Rob Gronkowski Set for Surgery." ESPN Boston. 7 January 2014. Web.

lxxiv Kyed, Doug. "Rob Gronkowski Not Participating in Patriots OTAs, 'Doing My Own Thing.'" NESN. 28 May 2014. Web.

lxxv "Bill Belichick: Rob Gronkowski Cleared to Play." CBS Boston. 23 July 2014. Web.

lxxvi "Dolphins Rally Past Patriots with Dominant 2nd Half." ESPN. 8 September 2014. Web.

lxxvii "Tom Brady Throws 5 TDs as Surging Patriots Crush Reeling

Bears." ESPN. 27 October 2014. Web.

[lxxviii] "Patriots Defense, Timely TD Help N.E. to 12th Straight 10-Win Season." ESPN. 8 December 2014. Web.

[lxxix] "Tom Brady Carries Pats to Rout of Colts, Claims Sixth Super Bowl Trip." ESPN. 19 January 2015. Web.

[lxxx] Orr, Connor. "Judge Nullifies Tom Brady's Four-Game Suspension." NFL.com. 4 September 2015. Web.

[lxxxi] "Healthy Gronkowski Ready to Roll in Super Bowl." WCVB.com. 27 January 2015. Web.

[lxxxii] MacMullan, Jackie. "Gronk Seeks Validation at SB XLIX." ESPN Boston. 29 January 2015. Web.

[lxxxiii] "Malcolm Butler's Goal-Line Interception Gives Pats Super Bowl XLIX Title." ESPN. 2 February 2015. Web.

[lxxxiv] "Four Players Slapped with Fines for Brawl at Super Bowl XLIX." *The Associated Press* (via Fox Sports). 6 February 2015. Web.

[lxxxv] "Super Bowl XLIX: Patriots Postgame Quotes." Patriots.com. 1 February 2015. Web.

[lxxxvi] Doyle, Ricky. "Rob Gronkowski Parties on Stage with Flo Rida after Super Bowl." NESN. 2 February 2015. Web.

[lxxxvii] Mandell, Nina. "Tom Brady Gronked Out at the Patriots' Super Bowl Ring Party." *USA Today*. 15 June 2015. Web.

[lxxxviii] "Tom Brady's 4 Passing TDs, 3 to Rob Gronkowski, Highlight Pats' Opening Win." ESPN. 11 September 2015. Web.

[lxxxix] "C.J. Anderson Scampers 48 Yards for TD to Ruin Pats' Unblemished Record." ESPN. 30 November 2015. Web.

[xc] Boren, Cindy. "The Patriots Made a Statement on Rob Gronkowski's Injury. Which is Weird." *The Washington Post*. 2 December 2015. Web.

[xci] "Tom Brady, Patriots Clinch Playoff Spot with Rout of Texans." ESPN. 14 December 2015. Web.

[xcii] "Rob Gronkowski Dedicates Game to Friend, Trainer who Passed Away This Week." CBS Boston. 20 December 2015. Web.

[xciii] "Pats Undaunted by Chiefs' Rally, Reach 5th Straight AFC Title Game." ESPN. 17 January 2016. Web.

[xciv] "NFL Team Total Defense Statistics – 2015." ESPN. Web.

[xcv] "NFL Team Total Offense Statistics – 2015." ESPN. Web.

xcvi "Broncos' Defense Stifles Patriots, Punches Ticket to Super Bowl 50." ESPN. 25 January 2016. Web.

xcvii "Patriots Postgame Quotes 1/24." Patriots.com. 25 January 2016. Web.

xcviii "Gronk: Partying Makes Me a Better Player." CBS News. 17 July 2015. Web.

xcix "A Night in the Life of Rob Gronkowski." *Esquire Magazine*. 15 July 2015. Web.

c Schwartz, Nick. "Johnny Manziel and Rob Gronkowski Partied by a Pool in Las Vegas." *USA Today*. 25 May 2014. Web.

ci "The Ultimate Gronk Experience!" TheGronkBus.com. Web.

cii McManaman, Bob. "Super Player of the Day: Patriots' Tight End Rob Gronkowski." AZ Central. 1 February 2015. Web.

ciii GronksPartyShip.com. Web.

civ Breech, John. "Look: Rob Gronkowski Bongs Beer in 'Entourage' Movie Preview." CBS Sports. 27 December 2014. Web.

cv Fischer, Jake. "Q&A: Rob Gronkowski Talks Training, His Role in Entourage and Much More." SI.com. 19 June 2015. Web.

cvi Grautski, Amara. "Patriots Tight End Rob Gronkowski Dodges DeflateGate Question, Twerks on 'Celebrity Family Feud.'" *New York Daily News*. 20 July 2015. Web.

cvii Fiske, Angelique. "Rob Gronkowski Named Host of Crashletes, New Nickelodeon Show." Patriots.com. 8 March 2016. Web.

cviii "Six Star Pro Nutrition Signs Multi-Year Endorsement Contracts with Three Top Pro Athletes." MuscleAndFitness.com. 29 February 2012. Web.

cix van der Pool, Lisa. "Dunkin' Signs 2-Year Sponsorship with Patriots' Gronkowski." *Boston Business Journal*. 27 March 2012. Web.

cx Madden, Lance. "Rob Gronkowski Becomes Endorser, Investor for BodyArmor Sports Drink." *Forbes Magazine*. 14 August 2012. Web.

cxi Rovell, Darren. "Gronk Flakes Hitting New England Shelves." ESPN. 22 September 202. Web.

cxii Edelman, Marc. "Illegal Procedure? Rob Gronkowski Endorses Two Daily Fantasy Sports Games in the Same Season." *Forbes Magazine*. 12 December 2014. Web.

cxiii "Rob Gronkowski Joins SMS Audio as Brand Ambassador."

ThisIsMelo.com. 17 January 2015. Web.

[cxiv] Rovell, Darren. "Patriots TE Rob Gronkowski Signs Multiyear Deal with Monster Drink." 21 November 2015. Web.

[cxv] Klemko, Robert. "How Do We Stop This from Happening?" MMQB.SI.com. 22 June 2015. Web.

[cxvi] GronkFitnessProducts.com. Web.

[cxvii] GronkNation.com/Foundation/

[cxviii] www.ProCamps.com/RobGronkowski

[cxix] Reiss, Mike. "Rob Gronkowski Set to Host Another Women's Football Clinic." ESPN Boston. 18 August 2015. Web.

[cxx] Breech, Jon. "Look: Rob Gronkowski Explains in Tweet Why he Doesn't Have a Girlfriend." CBS Sports. 27 February 2015. Web.

[cxxi] Keeney, Tim. "Camille Kostek, Rob Gronkowski's Girlfriend: The Pictures You Need to See." Heavy.com. 29 October 2015. Web.

[cxxii] Goldstein, Meredith. "Camille Kostek Talks Benrus and Rob Gronkowski." *The Boston Globe*. 29 April 2015. Web.

[cxxiii] Greer, Carlos. "Is Rob Gronkowski Losing His Ex-Cheerleader Girlfriend?" PageSix.com. 17 January 2016. Web.

[cxxiv] Nessif, Bruna and Machado, Baker. "NFL Hunk Rob Gronkowski Reveals his Valentine's Day Plans (and if There's Someone Special!)." E! News. 2 February 2016. Web.

Made in the USA
Columbia, SC
12 May 2020